CARL SAGAN,
ASTRONOMER AND
PLANETARY SCIENTIST

IMAGINATION WILL OFTEN CARRY US TO WORLDS THAT NEVER WERE. BUT WITHOUT IT WE GO NOWHERE.

CREATIVELY HUMAN

WHY WE IMAGINE, MAKE AND INNOVATE

LOIS PETERSON

ILLUSTRATED BY

MADELINE YEE

ORCA BOOK PUBLISHERS

Published in Canada and the United States in 2025 by Orca Book Publishers.
orcabook.com

Library and Archives Canada Cataloguing in Publication
Title: Creatively human : why we imagine, make and innovate / Lois Peterson ; illustrated by Madeline Yee.
Names: Peterson, Lois, 1952- author. | Yee, Madeline, illustrator.
Series: Orca think ; 18.
Description: Series statement: Orca think ; 18 | Includes bibliographical references and index.
Identifiers: Canadiana (print) 2024037052X | Canadiana (ebook) 20240370538 | ISBN 9781459837775 (hardcover) | ISBN 9781459837782 (PDF) | ISBN 9781459837799 (EPUB)
Subjects: LCSH: Creative ability—Juvenile literature. | LCSH: Creative thinking—Juvenile literature. | LCSH: Imagination—Juvenile literature. | LCSH: Creative ability—Social aspects—Juvenile literature. | LCSH: Creative thinking—Social aspects—Juvenile literature. | LCSH: Imagination—Social aspects—Juvenile literature. | LCGFT: Informational works.
Classification: LCC BF723.C7 P48 2025 | DDC j153.3/5—dc23

Library of Congress Control Number: 2024936681

Summary: Part of the nonfiction Orca Think series, this illustrated book for middle-grade readers explores creativity and how it affects our lives and our world.

Orca Book Publishers is committed to reducing the consumption of nonrenewable resources in the production of our books. We make every effort to use materials that support a sustainable future.

Orca Book Publishers gratefully acknowledges the support for its publishing programs provided by the following agencies: the Government of Canada, the Canada Council for the Arts and the Province of British Columbia through the BC Arts Council and the Book Publishing Tax Credit.

Cover and interior artwork by Madeline Yee.
Design by Troy Cunningham.
Edited by Kirstie Hudson.

Printed and bound in South Korea.

28 27 26 25 • 1 2 3 4

This book is dedicated to anyone who ever said, "Me? I'm not creative!" And to everyone who helps us celebrate the creativity we find inside ourselves and share with the world.

CONTENTS

CHAPTER SIX: THE WAY WE SEE IT

CHAPTER SEVEN: CHANGING OURSELVES AND OUR WORLD

CHAPTER EIGHT: GOOD, BETTER, BEST

CONTENTS

INTRODUCTION

On a recent beach walk, I met two classes of students from the nearby elementary school. They had come to "plant" hand-painted kindness rocks among the sand, shells and logs. The idea of making decorated rocks to cheer people up originated in 2015 when a woman in Cape Cod, Maine, placed a rock on her local beach. On it she had painted the words *You've got this!*

The practice of decorating stones with pictures or messages soon grew and spread. Then, during the early days of the COVID-19 pandemic in 2020, people's freedom to spend time together was limited. Like many other kids, you might have started placing hand-painted kindness rocks in your yard for passing pedestrians and drivers to see. This simple creative activity spread joy at a time when many people were lonely and afraid. And it was a great way for caring people to express themselves creatively.

Kindness rocks are now a common sight in yards, parks and other private and public places.
KIMBERLEE REIMER/GETTY IMAGES

IN THE BEGINNING

My father, a teacher by profession, wrote about his life, acted in plays, sketched and made up funny songs. My mother made quilts and embroidered. My sister created papier-mâché bowls and clocks. When we were children, she played piano, my brother played the violin and I played the cello. Today I write books and articles. And I am learning to paint and make collages. If you listed all the things that your family and friends love to do and make, you might be surprised at how creative you all are. You are doing what all humans do in one way or another—approaching the world creatively, hoping to make it a better place for yourself and others.

In writing this book, I wanted to know:

- why the human urge to make and create is so strong;
- who benefits from our creative efforts—and how;
- how the world is made better by our instinct to express ourselves and change our world;
- what helps us do what we want to do—and do it well; and
- where we display, perform or enjoy creative work.

This papier-mâché clock has been keeping time since my sister made it 30 years ago.
LOIS PETERSON

A survey of 1,500 workplace leaders showed that creativity was the top quality required of senior staff in their companies. I discovered that a discussion hosted by the Canadian Network for Imagination and Creativity was being led by a custodial supervisor for an Ontario school board—the person who works with janitors and maintenance staff.

Creativity really *is* everywhere! Everyone *is* creative!

"Creativity is intelligence having fun."

Albert Einstein, one of the world's most famous scientists

Cardboard boxes offer lots of ways to imagine, make and innovate.
MOMO PRODUCTIONS/GETTY IMAGES

chapter one

WHAT IS CREATIVITY?

The potential for creativity *is* in all of us, even if we don't recognize it ourselves. For example, Arushi Shailendra made her first painting when she was only four months old. Now a young adult, this Indian artist has made thousands. Her artwork has been exhibited in several shows, and she has won numerous awards.

When they have time before school in the morning, Sloane and Fletcher build sandcastles at their local beach.

LOIS PETERSON

EVERYONE CAN DO IT

What do a hazmat suit, a face shield and an allergy-detection device have in common? They were invented by teen siblings Mark, Gary and Barbara Leschinsky of New Jersey. They are just three of the many young inventors whose achievements are celebrated every year on January 17, Kid Inventors' Day.

In 1943 US Navy engineer Richard James accidentally invented the Slinky when he noticed how a spring moved across the floor after he dropped it. Since then 30 million Slinkies have been sold.

DOING WHAT COMES NATURALLY

Creativity is part of our lives from very early on—a universal instinct to sing, dance, scribble, dig in the sand, dress up. Even if we don't remember doing it. Most of us—wherever we live, whatever our culture or religion, the language we speak or our gender—approach the world creatively. You make

Choosing what to wear may be the first of many creative things we do each day, whether we realize it or not.
MIXMIKE/GETTY IMAGES

creative decisions every day, from the moment you get up to when you go to bed. Even if you don't realize it at the time.

One definition of creativity is "the ability to create or imagine something new and original." But there are about as many ways to describe it as there are people in the world. Creativity is such an important part of human life that the United Nations named April 21 World Creativity and Innovation Day.

GREAT MINDS THINK ALIKE

In Sicily a museum is dedicated to the work of two men, scientist Archimedes (287 to 211 or 212 BCE) and artist/inventor/scientist Leonardo da Vinci (1452 to 1519). The Archimedes and Leonardo Museum in Syracuse displays machines and contraptions that grew out of these men's minds and imaginations. Of course, the two never met, living more than 1,000 years apart. Yet they shared the same spirit of creativity, exploration and discovery.

Archimedes is perhaps most famous for discovering why objects float or sink when they are immersed in water. He discovered this while he was taking a bath and thinking of other things. Even though it never flew, Leonardo da Vinci invented a flying machine called the ornithopter 400 years before the Wright Brothers took their 1903 flight in the *Wright Flyer* near Kitty Hawk, North Carolina. Leonardo used his artistic skills, mechanical knowledge and visionary ideas to make drawings and notes of other artistic, technological and scientific advances that were far beyond his time.

The innovative ideas of these two men have inspired inventors, artists and dreamers to push the boundaries of what we know, imagine and create. We might call Archimedes and Leonardo scientists, artists, inventors or visionaries. But at the heart of their work was the desire to use their creativity to explore, shape and imagine the world.

This young girl reacts spontaneously to how the music makes her feel.
MOMO PRODUCTIONS/GETTY IMAGES

You don't have to paint a masterpiece, create worldbuilding video games, perform on a New York stage, have your name on the spine of a book, create a bestselling toy or invent a life-changing device to be considered creative. You already are, by virtue of being human. Examples are all around you. At home. In the places you share and those where you spend time alone. Wherever you interact with others. It's in what you do and wear, what you watch, read, listen to, talk about and explore. It's in the tools you use, the ones you invent, and how you use them. The creative activities of everyone contribute so much to our world. And so much of our lives is affected by the creativity of others.

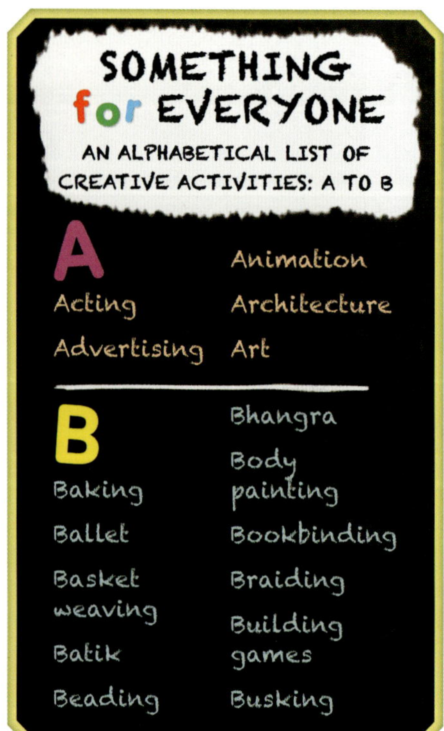

LEARNING OUR OWN WAY

Some creative skills come to us naturally. Others we learn and develop with a specific goal in mind. And sometimes we do creative things just for the fun of it. Not everyone learns the same way. Some people do better "under their own steam." They seek out information and practice what they have learned in private. Some learn by watching others. Some people need a teacher and benefit from learning one-on-one. And others learn best in a group of people doing the same thing, where they can share and learn from each other. Most people learn something new through a combination of methods.

It is hard to imagine the time before the internet gave people with similar interests a place to learn, share or hang out with others exploring the same things.

WHY ARE WE CREATIVE?

Creativity allows us to:

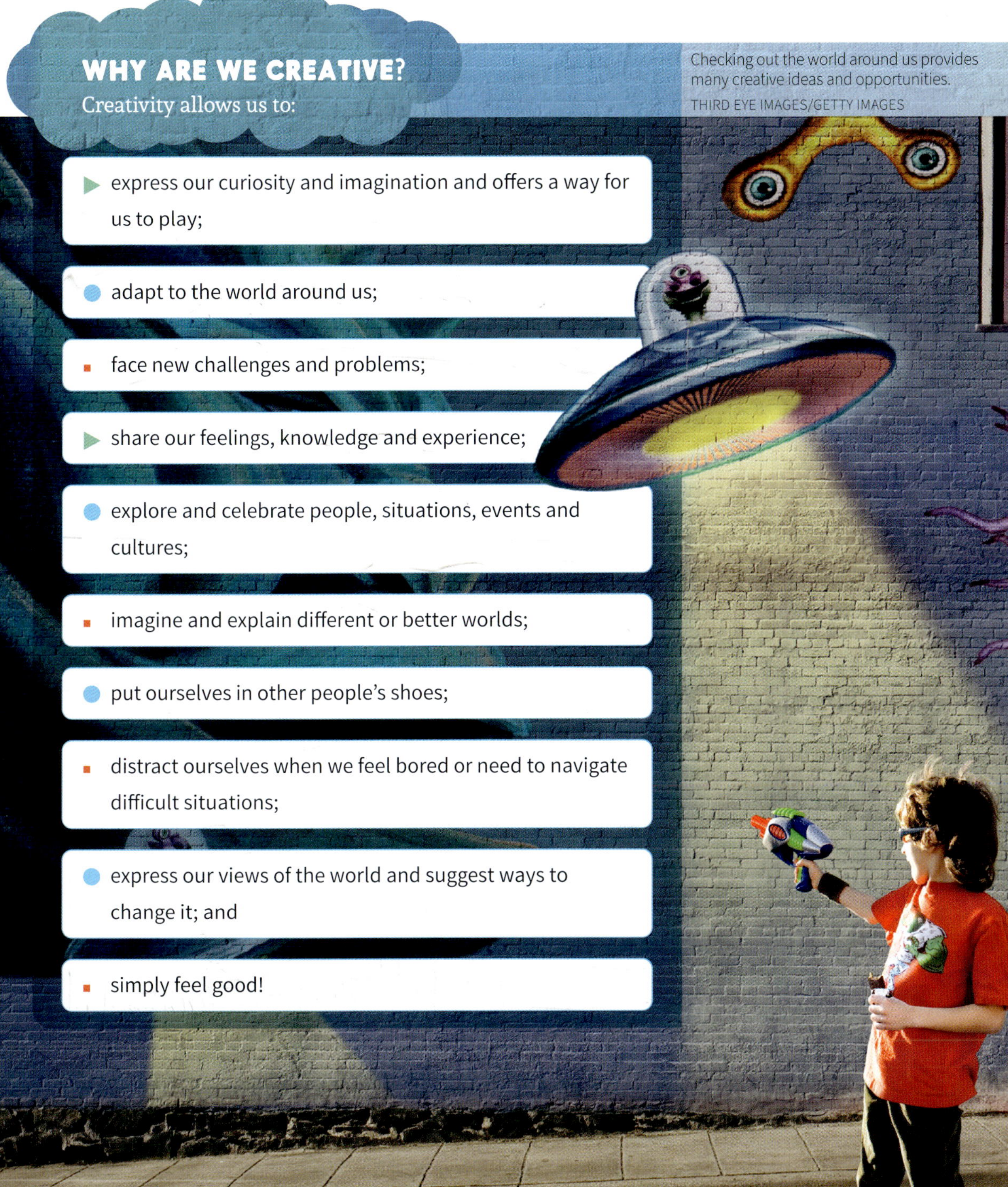

- express our curiosity and imagination and offers a way for us to play;
- adapt to the world around us;
- face new challenges and problems;
- share our feelings, knowledge and experience;
- explore and celebrate people, situations, events and cultures;
- imagine and explain different or better worlds;
- put ourselves in other people's shoes;
- distract ourselves when we feel bored or need to navigate difficult situations;
- express our views of the world and suggest ways to change it; and
- simply feel good!

Checking out the world around us provides many creative ideas and opportunities.
THIRD EYE IMAGES/GETTY IMAGES

On platforms like YouTube, Zoom and TikTok, artists demonstrate their skills. Writers get together to read and offer suggestions on each other's work. Visual artists demonstrate techniques. Actors perform or rehearse together. Singers train with a teacher or practice with other choir members. Right now, all over the world, people are coming up with even more ways to connect, learn and share interests and skills.

NEVER TOO SOON—OR TOO LATE

Although our creative instincts are strong, not everyone has the opportunity, support or resources they need to reach their full potential. But once someone finds something they love doing—writing songs, doing mime, designing clothes—they might study formally in school or college and make a career of doing what they love. Or they might just continue doing it for their own enjoyment.

There are many stories of older people picking up a paintbrush, writing a novel, acting in local theater or learning the drums for the first time. Canadian author Gordon Korman wrote his first book, *This Can't Be Happening at Macdonald Hall*, when he was just 12. Decades later he is still writing, and his books have sold 30 million copies worldwide. The saying "It's never too late" (or "You're never too young") truly applies to any creative activity.

CHANGING ATTITUDES AND IDEAS

Like most things in life, ideas about the origins and purpose of creativity have changed over time.

The Greek ***philosopher*** Aristotle believed that the brain had nothing to do with creativity. It was only a thermostat, keeping our blood at the right temperature.

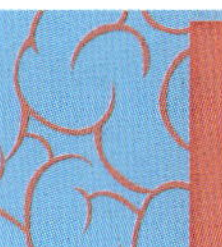

In medieval times it was thought that the purpose of human creativity was to please a divine god.

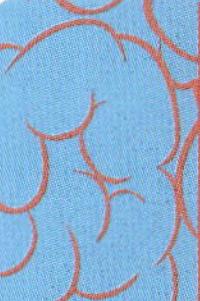

During the ***Renaissance*** (14th to 17th centuries) it was believed that creativity reflected the human desire to voice a sense of freedom and self-expression.

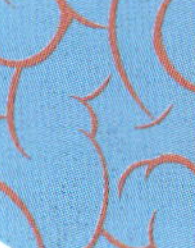

In the 19th century it was thought that creativity applied only to the creation of art.

In the 20th century creativity was reflected in both visual and performance art.

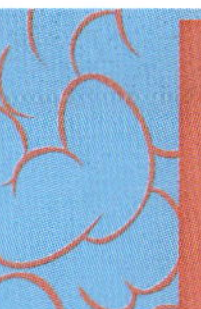

Later we became aware of how creative thinking can apply to the study of science and that we could use science to express creativity.

The first research into the effect of creativity on our minds and moods was done in 1950, less than 80 years ago.

In 2015 a professor of psychology was the first scientist to suggest that the part of the brain called the frontal cortex is most involved in our creativity. With many people working in the field of brain science and creativity, we are bound to continue learning about this incredible organ and its role in our creative lives.

FROM PIGMENTS TO PUPPETRY TO PERSONAL COMPUTERS

Over time we have adopted and adapted for creative use many items and practices that originally had a more practical purpose.

Woven fabric and plant material have been used for practical, ceremonial and decorative purposes for more than 12,000 years. A piece of woven carpet found near Konya, Turkey, in 1905 is thought to be 9,000 years old.

The potter's wheel, invented about 5,000 years ago to make cups, bowls and dishes, is now used for decorative items too. Wheels that were originally operated by hand or foot are now often mechanically driven or even solar-powered.

Paintbrushes were invented in China about 2,500 years ago.

The 17,000-year-old paintings in the Lascaux Cave in France include pigments, natural coloring matter made from animals and plants. Ancient peoples added color to wall paintings and dyed their clothing and hair for cultural and religious reasons.

Tattoos have decorated bodies and reflected cultural values and personal experience since at least 3400–3100 BCE.

Beads and buttons were probably first used for counting and decorative purposes. Two-thousand-year-old beads made of clay and bone have been found in Israel and Algeria.

One of the early ways for people to share stories was using puppets made of wood, animal skin or fabric. A puppet of a cow with a moving head, dating back about 2,000 years, was found in the Indus Valley in India.

In about 1030, Guido de Arezzo was the first person to document music so that it could be reproduced note for note by other musicians.

The first movable-type printing press was invented by Johannes Gutenberg around 1440. He could never have imagined that one day people would print their own stories at home!

The piano was invented around 1700 as an improvement on the harpsichord.

Regardless of how we create and produce music, choosing the first note of a new piece of music is always exciting.
HILL STREET STUDIOS/GETTY IMAGES

A single picture, taken using the camera obscura, an early form of the camera, took eight hours to develop.

Multitrack recording was developed in the 1940s. It allows many tracks of music to be recorded individually and then mixed together to create a full sound.

Computers have been used for business and storing information since about 1950. Home video games came into use in about 1966. Word processors have been a great help to writers since one called The Electric Pencil was introduced in 1976. Not long after, the use of computers for graphics and animation was developed.

"Artificial intelligence (AI) creativity is like having a robot that can make cool things like a human artist! It uses special algorithms and computer programs to analyze patterns and generate new ideas. AI can help create music, paintings, stories and even games. It's like having a super-powered assistant who can help you think of new ideas and create things faster than you ever could on your own." This paragraph was written in 2023 by the AI program Chat GPT. Whether AI-generated writing, art and other creative work is authentic and legitimate is a hotly debated topic in creative communities.

Whoever we are, whatever we do, we can all make a difference to the world. All it takes is a little creativity! Born in Churchill, Manitoba, and raised in Nunavut in northern Canada, Susan Aglukark blends music and rhythms from her Inuk culture with folk and pop music. The first musician of Inuk heritage to win a Juno Award (she has now won three), Aglukark uses her music to share her cultural heritage, language and traditional music. In the process she brings attention to social issues, including abuse and suicide, that disproportionately affect Indigenous Peoples in Canada. Susan writes and sings in both English and Inuktitut. Some of her music features throat singing, which she teaches Inuk youth to help keep Inuit cultural traditions alive.

Susan Aglukark
Singer

chapter two

OUR BRAINS AND BODIES

Most of us come by natural talents (for music, sports, art, etc.) through a combination of our genes—traits and characteristics passed down by our parents—and the culture and environment around us. But if we have ideas of what we want to do and achieve, we have to work hard and practice to develop the specific skills we need.

This dancer's vibrant performance conveys their pride and joy in their culture.
PHOTOSBYJIM/GETTY IMAGES

GETTING STARTED

The child watching their parents carve pictures into a cave wall 50,000 years ago might have then picked up a rock to create their own artwork. Learning by imitation is often a good start. From the time we are born, we react to music, clap and wave,

SOMETHING for EVERYONE

AN ALPHABETICAL LIST OF CREATIVE ACTIVITIES: C

C

Cake decorating
Calligraphy
Candle making
Candy making
Carpentry
Cartooning
Carving wood and stone
Choreography
Collage
Coloring
Comedy
Comic-book art and writing
Cooking
Cosplay
Creative writing
Crochet
Cross-stitch

scribble and scrawl, dance and play, imagine and build—no matter our gender, background or culture. When we see something we like, we often want to do it too.

BUILT FOR CREATIVITY

One of the most spectacular videos I ran across recently was by a group based in Italy, called Urban Theory. They perform mesmerizing dances in the tutting style, which involves making shapes and angles with their limbs, hands and fingers. A number of attributes help humans be more creative than dogs or goldfish:

1. **OPPOSABLE THUMBS**: They allow you to pick up and manipulate things, from paintbrushes and carpentry tools to sewing needles and a conductor's baton.

2. **FLEXIBLE HANDS**: Made up of 27 bones, your hands are useful for handling tools and for gesturing in dance, theater and mime. The fingers of a classically trained Indian dancer convey story, emotion and drama.

A violinist's hands are as complex and delicate as their instrument.
CAVAN IMAGES/GETTY IMAGES

3. **EYES**: Two visual powers allow you to appreciate what you see around you.

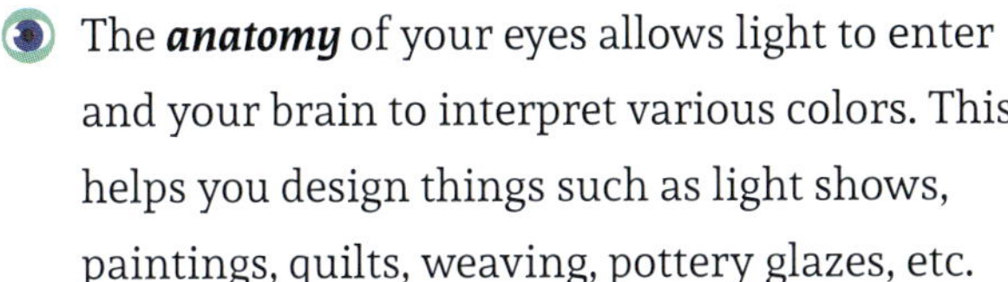

- The ***anatomy*** of your eyes allows light to enter and your brain to interpret various colors. This helps you design things such as light shows, paintings, quilts, weaving, pottery glazes, etc.

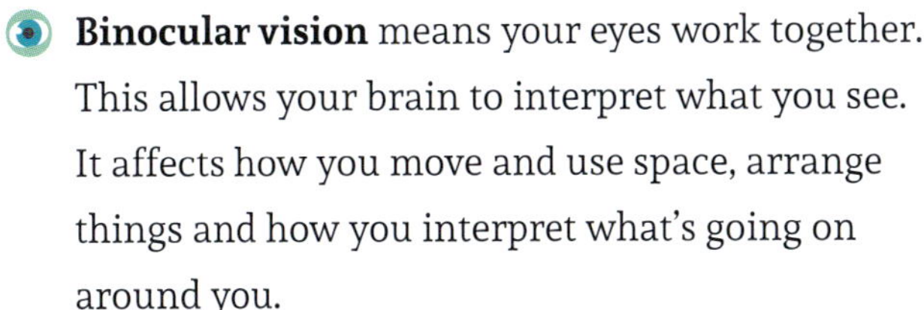

- **Binocular vision** means your eyes work together. This allows your brain to interpret what you see. It affects how you move and use space, arrange things and how you interpret what's going on around you.

Studying these paintings might encourage this boy to pick up a paintbrush himself—or offer him a new way to look at the world.
U.OZEL.IMAGES/GETTY IMAGES

It would have taken years of training for this young performer to reach this level of skill.
JACOB WACKERHAUSEN/GETTY IMAGES

BODY: You can train your body to move and perform in ways that might not be entirely natural but that enhance your creative work.

BRAIN: Your complex brain allows you to analyze, imagine, dream and plan.

- The **FRONTAL CORTEX** controls much of what you do when you are being creative.
- The **HIPPOCAMPUS** stores and retrieves information to help you remember what you have learned.
- The **BASAL GANGLIA** supports muscle memory.
- The **WHITE MATTER** connects parts of your brain that need to work together for many creative activities.

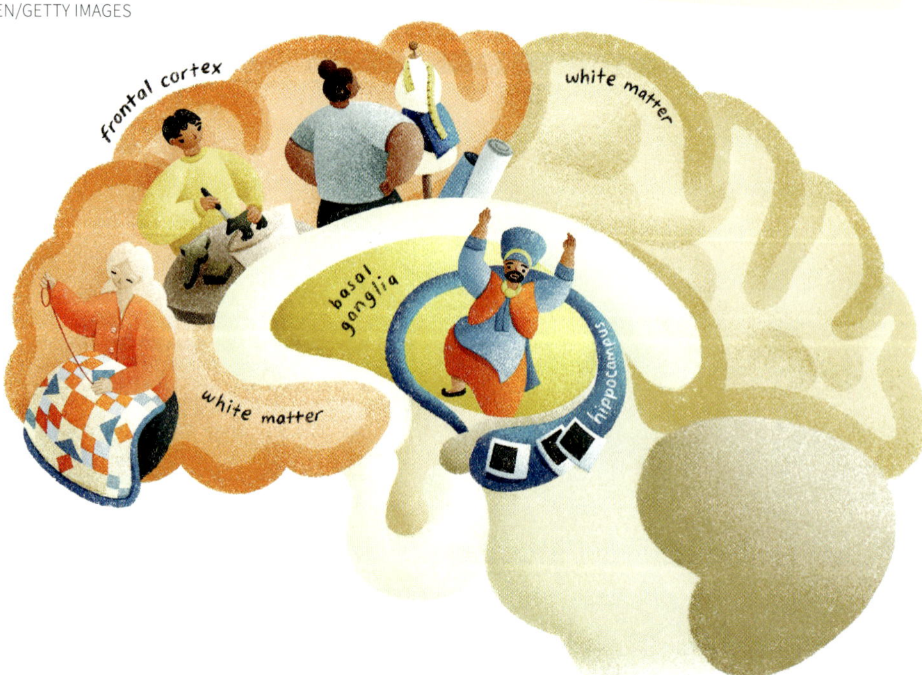

The debate about how the two sides of our brains work has been going on for a long time. But it is thought that the right brain controls how you manage the space around you and process images and music. The left brain is more involved in technical things like math, music and using logic.

6. **COOPERATION**: Like other creatures, humans work together. We exchange ideas, build on them using input from others, bring individual skills to a shared project and celebrate everyone's accomplishments.

BRAIN POWER

A Greek physician named Galen was the first to suggest that different parts of the brain manage thought, control our bodily functions and are responsible for how memory works. And he thought that the ability to imagine and create originated in our hearts.

Many traditional arts, such as Japanese bonsai, are passed down through the generations.
KAREN MOSKOWITZ/GETTY IMAGES

We certainly know that making art, singing or dancing "wholeheartedly" makes the activity more enjoyable for ourselves and for those watching or seeing our work. But scientific knowledge about our brains and how they work has changed over time—and keeps changing.

We now know that different parts of our brains control different areas of our physical bodies, our emotions and our thinking. And that thinking, making and creating can actually change the structure of our brains and how they work. As we get older, our brains age too, affecting how we control our bodies and use our minds. So things we could once do easily often get more challenging. Continuing to create all our lives—or even taking up something new like dancing, singing or art in later life—helps keep our brains healthy longer.

You may find that exercising your creativity improves your concentration and mood. Practicing something over and over helps you do even better next time. Taking pride in achieving your goals gives you confidence that you can manage other challenges and new situations. And doing things together—painting, performing in a play, singing in a choir—can make everyone feel good.

WHAT DOES IT TAKE?

A number of human qualities help us be creative:

- A sense of play, whether we are six or 96.
- The ability to be alone. Many people find this time useful for thinking about problems, coming up with solutions, exploring new ideas and options.
- Willingness to try new things, take chances and experiment.
- The ***psychological*** ability to turn difficult situations into more positive ones.
- Being sensitive to emotions and feelings—our own and other people's.
- Being comfortable in thinking differently than others.
- Approaching tasks and challenges from various angles without worrying about whether we're right.
- Using intuition—acting on feelings and reactions as well as on facts and information.

Muscle memory means that once you have learned something physical—turning clay on a potter's wheel, learning dance moves, braiding friendship bracelets—your brain allows you to do the action without having to think about which muscle to move, when and how. That's where the common phrase "Practice makes perfect" comes from.

LET'S DANCE

Dancing comes to us naturally when we're young, and it can be a freeing and pleasurable activity for people of all ages. Sometimes we need formal training. Or we might do it spontaneously to express our feelings. Whether we make up steps on the spot or follow specific movements, dancing can lift our spirits and help our mental health. Dance has always been important in our cultural and recreational life.

CAVE ART dating back thousands of years often depicts people dancing.

DRAGON DANCES, a traditional form of Chinese dance dating back more than 2,000 years, was originally used to communicate with the ancestors and appeal for good weather.

THE WALTZ developed in Austria and Germany in the 13th century and soon spread to other countries. These days TV shows such as *Dancing with the Stars* and *Strictly Come Dancing* are popular all over the world.

Pointe shoes are specially reinforced to allow dancers to balance on their toes. But years of dancing in them can damage the feet.
NISIAN HUGHES/GETTY IMAGES

BHANGRA is a traditional dance of the Punjab region of India. It is one of the dances often featured in Bollywood movies, which have melodramatic plots and exuberant music, singing and dancing.

BALLET was introduced into the Italian royal court in about 1500. Four hundred years later, one of history's most famous dancers, Anna Pavlova, introduced the modern pointe shoe. These allow female dancers to dance on their toes.

TAP DANCING combines traditional Irish dance of the 19th century with the rhythmic dancing of slave workers in the American south.

FLAMENCO was originally performed by the Romani peoples of Europe.

MODERN DANCE originated in Europe and the United States in the late 1800s. It expresses human emotions through movement, in a theatrical, unstructured form.

BREAKDANCING combines martial arts and gymnastics. It was introduced by African American, Latino and Hispanic dancers in New York in the late 1960s and early '70s.

FLEXING (sometimes spelled FlexN) is a street dance that originated in Brooklyn, New York, in the 1990s.

Whether you do it in private or public, dancing is a powerful form of creative expression.
WESTEND61/GETTY IMAGES

Born in a farming family in the Punjab area of India, Gurdeep Pandher moved to Canada in 2006. After becoming a Canadian citizen in 2011, he was inspired to travel across the country to learn more about his new home. He lived in a number of places before settling in Yukon, where he works as a writer and speaker encouraging cross-cultural understanding. But he may be most widely known as a dancer, energetically and joyfully combining traditional Indian bhangra with other forms of dance, which he shares with people all over the country, both in person and on his YouTube videos and in community activities.

Gurdeep Pandher
Dancer

ASHLEY SWINTON PHOTOGRAPHY

A MATTER OF TASTE

We don't all enjoy the same kind of music or art, laugh at the same things, like the same style of clothes or want the same flowers in a bouquet. Some of the differences in our tastes are due to a part of the brain called the medial frontal cortex. It analyzes the qualities of a piece of art, a song or a play and decides whether they are pleasing to us or not, just as it decides whether we like or dislike bananas or liver, striped clothes or polka-dotted.

Where you live, what you're exposed to, and where your talents lie also affect what you appreciate and enjoy. So it's fortunate that there are so many different forms of art, music, dance, fashion and furniture for us to enjoy.

chapter three

SPACES AND PLACES

Ever since ancient people gathered around the fire to tell stories, or ancient Roman poets recited on street corners, open spaces have been used for performances and exhibits. For centuries, traveling entertainers roamed Europe and Asia, performing plays and singing songs that reflected the lives of ordinary people and poked fun at the wealthy. In North America, during the late 19th and early 20th centuries, traveling performers in the Chautauqua movement put on tent shows, bringing learning, culture and entertainment to small towns and villages for a few days at a time. Throughout history, artists have used sidewalks and walls as their canvases, creating pictures of famous people or historical scenes where everyone can see them.

This juggler is carrying on a long tradition of public performance.
WESTEND61/GETTY IMAGES

HERE, THERE AND EVERYWHERE

Artists, actors, dancers and musicians all over the world perform and exhibit in many different venues, including some rather unlikely places.

In 2014, as part of an art exhibit in London, England, the band Unfathomable Ruination performed in an airtight box. Bands have performed in storefront windows, at the top of a ski jump in Sweden and in a salt mine in Germany.

The most unusual opera house might be in Manaus, Brazil, a city in the middle of the Amazon jungle.

Every year since 2016, a group of Egyptian women called Art D'Egypte have staged ***modern art*** exhibitions at various Egyptian heritage sites, including the 4,500-year-old Pyramids of Giza.

The strangest place to promote writing and art might be The Bower, a ***feminist*** gallery located in a converted public bathroom and park-keeper's hut in Camberwell, London.

The Eric Whitacre Virtual Choir—as many as 7,500 singers aged 4 to 87, from 120 countries—perform online without having met or rehearsed in person.

Actors continue to perform on the stage of London's new Globe Theatre, a replica of the venue where many of Shakespeare's plays were performed in the 1600s.

KAMIRA/SHUTTERSTOCK.COM

Actors perform historical plays in the vaults underneath the Edinburgh Central Library.

Dancers have performed in a giant aquarium and high in the rigging of a ship.

The works of William Shakespeare, the world's most famous playwright, have been performed on an airplane, in a cemetery and in a hospital, among other places.

After reading about this artist, you might think twice next time you spot—or spit—a blob of gum on the sidewalk. In London, Ben Wilson, known as the Pavement Picasso, converts discarded gum into sidewalk masterpieces. He uses a blowtorch to soften each one, sprays it with lacquer, then creates a design with acrylic paint. He leaves his masterpieces on the sidewalk for everyone to admire.

Wilson also carves in wood, sculpts, paints and creates collages from litter. His work has been displayed in galleries in England, the United States, Germany, Ireland, Finland and France. His sidewalk activities sometimes draw a crowd, which attracts the notice of the police. But as he's not defacing public property, he's free to continue creating his unique kind of art out of the things pedestrians can't be bothered to throw into the garbage.

BEN WILSON

Ben Wilson
Chewing-Gum Artist

FLASH MOBS

You may have seen people gathering and breaking into song on the street or at the mall. Flash mobs bring performers together publicly in a way that looks natural and surprising. The first flash mob broke out in New York City in 2003. Since then they have popped up in airports, on city streets, on sports fields, in train stations—anywhere people gather. Created to look spontaneous, the performances are usually carefully planned and ***choreographed*** to draw attention to an upcoming theater performance or concert. Or they may be another way for performers to do what they love to do, sharing dance and music with people who might not otherwise have the chance to see them.

Every year Michael Jackson fans gather all over the world to sing and dance to his hit "Thriller." In 2007, 1,722 dancers on five continents broke a Guinness World Record when they participated in the Thrill the World flash mob. Some laws prohibit people from gathering for public activities of any kind. But the constitutions of many countries protect most public performances under people's right to gather peacefully.

The Minack Theatre on Cornwall's south coast is only one of many unusual settings for plays, concerts, musicals and exhibits.

TBRADFORD/GETTY IMAGES

EVERYWHERE FOR EVERYONE

How many people can you fit in a phone booth? The answer is two, if you are visiting the green phone box in a village in County Durham, England—one of the smallest art galleries in the world. There are about 19,000 art galleries across 124 countries worldwide, displaying sculptures, paintings, prints, multimedia exhibits, drawings and ***artifacts***. People have displayed their art in places as varied as an old police station, a public washroom, subway cars and an old printing factory.

BUILDING A CLIFF-TOP THEATER

Some of the most spellbinding times in my childhood were spent with my grandmother at the Minack Theatre in Cornwall, England. In the 1920s Rowena Cade moved to Cornwall where she hosted small plays in the garden of her house. In the 1940s, during the Second World War, with only a wheelbarrow and one other person to help her, she began to carve a spectacular outdoor theater on her land above Porthcurno Beach.

The Minack Theatre now attracts thousands of tourists and theater lovers each year. Its stage and performance areas have been enlarged, seating cut into the rocks has been improved, and a visitor center displays Cade's story. The theater's main appeal continues to be its spectacular setting. Cliffs, soaring seabirds and the sea form a dramatic background for plays and concerts.

James Harry and Lauren Brevner's Vancouver mural titled "Dreamweaver." Public art often reflects society's increasing awareness of the importance of diversity in everything we experience and are exposed to.

WIRESTOCK/ DREAMSTIME.COM

PUBLIC ART PROGRAMS

Many cities and towns now formally include some type of art in public buildings, often made by local creators and selected by city officials. These might be sculptures, wall gardens, paintings or architectural elements. In 2021 three banners by Kainai artist Kalum Teke Dan were hung in the atrium of the Calgary Municipal Building. Part of the Indigenous Placekeeping Program, they were displayed there until the end of 2023.

Public art can sometimes be controversial. Some people have objected to what they see as sexual or religious overtones in *Harmony*, a piece in Boynton Beach, Florida, by Patti Warashina. The 12-foot (3.6-meter) sculpture depicts a woman sitting atop a huge sphere, a conductor's baton in one hand and a musical note in the other, as if she's conducting the music of the world.

Informal art pops up in all kinds of venues all over the world for the benefit of local residents and tourists. You can track it on apps such as Street

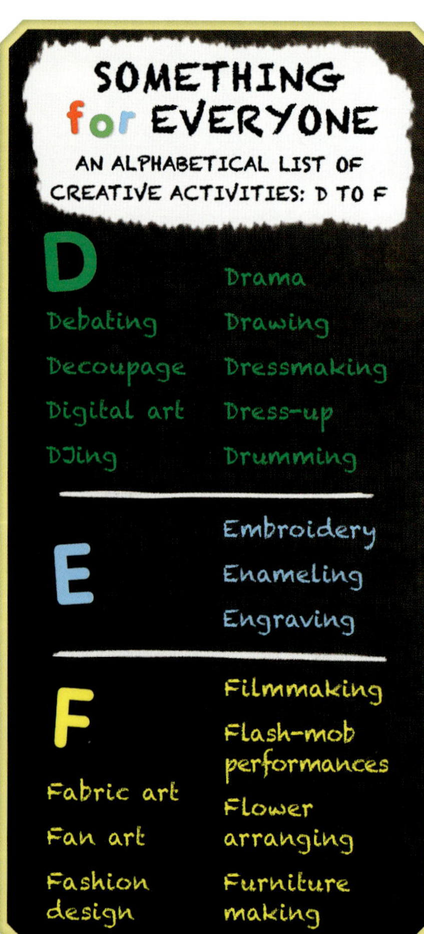

SOMETHING for EVERYONE

AN ALPHABETICAL LIST OF CREATIVE ACTIVITIES: D TO F

D

Debating
Decoupage
Digital art
DJing
Drama
Drawing
Dressmaking
Dress-up
Drumming

E

Embroidery
Enameling
Engraving

F

Fabric art
Fan art
Fashion design
Filmmaking
Flash-mob performances
Flower arranging
Furniture making

Art Cities, which in early 2024 listed 51,600 artworks in 1,440 cities in 100 countries.

We all bring our own taste to what we enjoy seeing, hearing or watching. But public art gives everyone the chance to see work they might not be exposed to otherwise. It also provides makers and creators with new venues to share their creativity.

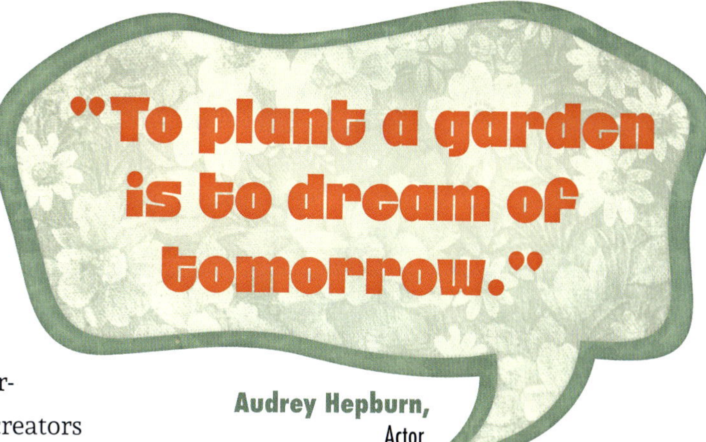

GRAFFITI—FROM SUBWAY CARS TO GALLERIES

Modern graffiti first appeared in Philadelphia in the early 1960s. ***Taggers*** were often members of street gangs, marking their territory. The practice soon spread to other cities, and it was not long before New York subway windows were so obscured by tags and images that passengers could not see out of them. In 1984 a big push to clean up the subway system forced graffiti artists to move their activities to buildings and rooftops. By then some New York galleries had started including graffiti in formal art shows. These exhibits became increasingly mainstream over the next 40 years.

Some people see graffiti as vandalism. Others appreciate it as a legitimate art form, bringing color and energy to city streets and public transit.

MARIOGUTI/GETTY IMAGES

ONLINE SPACES

Before the internet, many people only attended plays, music and art that were close to home, on TV or at local theaters. But now we enjoy much of it on demand at home. By 2022 more than 200 museums and galleries had put exhibits and collections online. Some, like New York's Metropolitan Museum, post performances of music and drama. New York's Lincoln Center for the Performing Arts films performances and posts them online. YouTube allows lovers of music, dance, art and drama to enjoy Japanese Kabuki, Nigerian Yoruba theater, Icelandic throat singing and all kinds of other performances they might not be able to see in their own communities. Artists and performers have access to much bigger audiences than ever before.

WRITTEN ON THE BODY

It might seem odd to think of our bodies as canvases or venues. But we use them every day for display, performance and self-expression.

FASHION

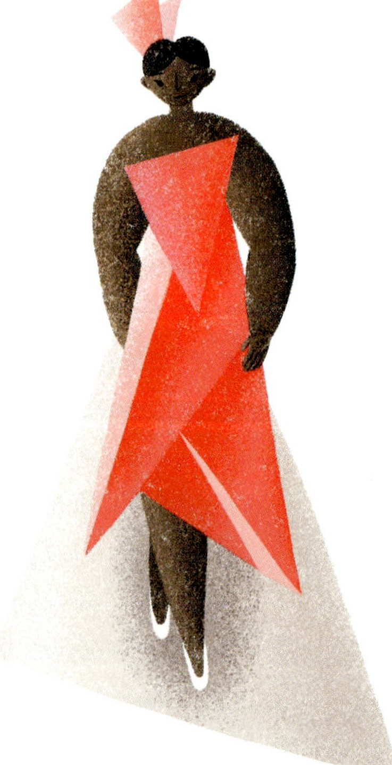

Few of us wear couture (high-end, custom-made) fashion. But the clothes you buy or choose to wear, and the way you dress, can say a lot about your personality, creativity and feelings. And fashion is not just for the young. Ari Seth Cohen's blog and film *Advanced Style* originally celebrated some of New York City's senior ***fashionistas.*** The project soon included fashion-conscious men and women in other American cities.

But the average American throws away about 82 pounds (37 kilograms) of clothing a year. In the United States alone,

TWO YOUNG FASHION BLOGGERS

TAVI GEVINSON started a fashion blog called *Style Rookie* when she was 12, later turning it into a now defunct online magazine called *Rookie*. Her interests have now grown to include theater and movies. She and her work have been featured in magazines such as the *New Yorker* and *Vogue*. Her developing skills demonstrate how interest in one creative activity often leads to others.

BRYANBOY started writing about fashion when he was a teen. By 2024 he had more than four million followers on TikTok and 900,000 on Instagram. He posts about fashion, makeup and fashion-related events, often modeling clothes himself.

more than 13 million tons (12 million metric tons) ends up in landfills annually, much of it is as good as new. Overproduction and overconsumption of clothing uses up valuable resources and energy. And the production and transportation of clothing is a major contributor to climate change. Thrifting, which involves exchanging unwanted items with friends or shopping at charity and consignment stores, is an approach to fashion that is more environmentally friendly and allows individual creativity to shine through. Some fashion lovers have learned to sew and dye so they can upcycle outdated items into new clothes, purses, wall hangings or rugs.

TATTOOS

Tattoos that resemble a mythical griffin were visible on the 2,500-year-old mummified body of the Siberian Ice Maiden, discovered in 1993 in Russia. Body tattoos have long been used to illustrate what is important in our lives. They feature images, words or names of people we admire or love.

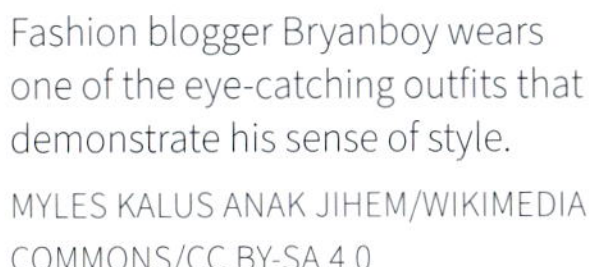

Fashion blogger Bryanboy wears one of the eye-catching outfits that demonstrate his sense of style.

MYLES KALUS ANAK JIHEM/WIKIMEDIA COMMONS/CC BY-SA 4.0

People use fashion, accessories and makeup to communicate individual creativity and personality.

FLASHPOP/GETTY IMAGES

They might promote political opinions or personal status. In some cultures, they convey religious beliefs or cultural connections. In the 1950s some children in Indiana and Arizona were tattooed with their blood type so they could be treated quickly in emergencies.

These days most tattoos are just for ornamentation. For adults in the western world, small tattoos—sometimes hidden by their clothes—are enough. Other people cover their entire bodies.

Here are other examples of how we use our bodies for creative expression:

Makeup has been around since the time of the Egyptians, when it was used to gain the attention of the gods.

Body piercing originated as a cultural practice in some African countries. In recent times, people with no specific cultural affiliation use piercing as ornament and personal expression.

I was about 14 when I got a very short hairstyle like those made famous by a 1960s fashion icon named Mary Quant. As an adult I have worn my long hair the same way for about 40 years. Some people like following trends, while others cut, shape and color their hair to express their own individuality.

Manicures, pedicures and nail art are popular for all ages.

I like to wear chunky necklaces, big earrings and a whole bunch of bangles. You might prefer more delicate chains, stud earrings or just one bead bracelet at a time. It's all a matter of personal taste.

OUR VERSATILE BODIES

Just as our bodies provide a canvas for personal creative expression, we also use our bodies to express creatively. Mime, in which not a word is spoken, depends on the expressiveness of the performer's body and face. Acting requires words, movement and gesture to create believable characters, situations and interactions. While some roles require creative costumes and makeup, others need only a simple tunic and bare feet to convey a story or emotion.

SHARING SPACE AND EQUIPMENT

In 1873 a sewing social club met in the Gowanda Free Library in New York State, which may have been the first example of a maker space. Today these shared spaces are increasingly popular in libraries, schools, art centers and other public venues. New and experienced artists, ***artisans*** and crafters work in the same place. Rather than each carpenter, painter, jeweler or sculptor needing their own tools, they may be shared communally. Sometimes they put on exhibitions of their work or sell what they produce on site. Some libraries lend out tools and musical instruments.

ALL AROUND THE HOUSE

Your bedroom decor and the things you keep around you probably convey your personality and interests.

The contents of your closet might reveal your own knitting and dressmaking skills or those of your family.

In many households, the fridge door exhibits the creative work of family members.

Watching TV may be the time you get cozy with blankets made by crafty family members or friends.

Family meals may showcase the creative efforts of the family cooks.

Your garden probably includes flowers, shrubs and trees chosen by the family gardener.

Paint colors, furniture and furnishings, the art on the walls and the ornaments on display reveal something of the tastes of everyone who lives in your house.

The clothes you wear and the things you have around you convey a lot about your personality and tastes.
PETER CADE/GETTY IMAGES

Wooden pallets used to ship goods all over the world are perfect for upcycling into sturdy outdoor furniture.

YULYAO/GETTY IMAGES

Not everyone owns their own home. So how we arrange furniture and what we keep around us also puts a creative "stamp" on where we live—something we can adapt if we move or our tastes and interests change.

Interior and landscape design are careers that many people with a creative flair pursue. Some take an ***ecological*** approach, using recycled materials or creating a new look from older furniture, fittings and other decorative elements.

ADVERTISING

Look around you! An organization called Common Sense Media estimates that we are each exposed to as many as 1,000 advertisements a day. They are used to sell us everything from coloring books to cosmetics, games to garden furniture, video games to vacations. Our phone and computer screens, billboards, shop signs, flyers, newspaper and magazine ads, posters plastered on buses, trains and telephone poles—all are vying for our attention, all of the time. In 2023 companies spent about $830 billion on advertising worldwide, and about 300,000 people in the United States alone work at coming up with creative ways to get consumers' attention. Advertising pops up wherever you are, wherever you go, in private, public or shared spaces. And its creation hinges on the skills and talents of artists, writers, musicians, animators, designers and producers. Once you start looking, you may be surprised at the amount and variety of work by creative people all around you.

PRINT

chapter four

TOOLS AND TECHNOLOGY

I was about seven when I decided to learn to paint. We had no TV, and there was no library or artist in our village. I was on my own. So my grandmother gave me a paint-by-number kit for my birthday.

Check out the Innovation Kids Lab's "Technology and Art" page on Pinterest. Browse the craft section of your school or public library. Visit your local hobby shop. You will discover many more ways to be creative and ways to share your work than I had when I was a kid.

Painting by numbers may not be as popular as it used to be, but it's still a great way to learn about color and create your own artworks.

MARIANA-RUSANOVSCHI/GETTY IMAGES

GETTING STARTED

We often start with what's available to us. Scribbling with paper and pencil. Building with DUPLO or LEGO sets. Helping Dad or Grandma decorate a cake. Then, as we get interested in other activities, we collect what we need. New and better materials, tools and technology constantly change the way we make,

create, collaborate, share and enjoy creative works of others.

Ancient humans used materials from their natural environment—earth, rock, vegetation, plant dyes, animal bones and hair. The things they used for art often began as tools and materials they used for everyday practical activities—stones, blades and other implements. And, like us, they also had their own bodies and voices for storytelling and singing.

This young musician is using an online tutorial to learn how to play the ukelele.
TDUB303/GETTY IMAGES

YOUTUBE

When I want to watch a painting tutorial, hear music by my favorite composer or learn how to decorate cupcakes, I often start by searching YouTube. Launched in 2005 by three former PayPal employees, YouTube was originally a place for people to post their own videos to share publicly. The first video was *Me at the Zoo*, posted on April 23, 2005, and shown in a tiny format. By 2023—less than 20 years later—there were as many as 800 million videos on YouTube. Many have been viewed millions of times. Others have been seen only by the creator's circle of friends and family.

On YouTube almost anyone can celebrate and share their own creativity—or enjoy the antics of baby goats in pajamas (my personal favorite). Classic movies, modern dance, craft demonstrations, cooking shows, exercise routines, hair-styling demos, nail-art demos and TV-show bloopers give anyone with an internet connection access to so much worldwide creativity.

Over time technology has helped us produce new and better tools, techniques and materials for our creative efforts, and more platforms for accessing it. Sometimes we only need to look around to find just what we need. And in many cases, we can make use of things that might otherwise have gone to waste.

THE POTENTIAL OF PAPER

A young girl who goes by the name Mayhem reproduces Oscar Award winners' gowns out of common products such as construction paper, gift wrap, tissue paper and foil. Some of the most beautiful sculptures I have seen are made out of cardboard—including realistic and life-sized wild animals—by Canadian artist Laurence Vallières.

Paper historians in England (there really *are* people whose job is to study this material we take for granted) figured out that we have developed more than 20,000 uses for paper. Many of them are familiar to us—books, flyers, posters, tickets, bookmarks, cardboard boxes, origami, paper-cutting, papier-mâché. Less common uses include sculpture and furniture making.

About four million hard-copy books are published each year. That's a lot of paper—and a lot of trees used in their production. And also many writers, editors and book

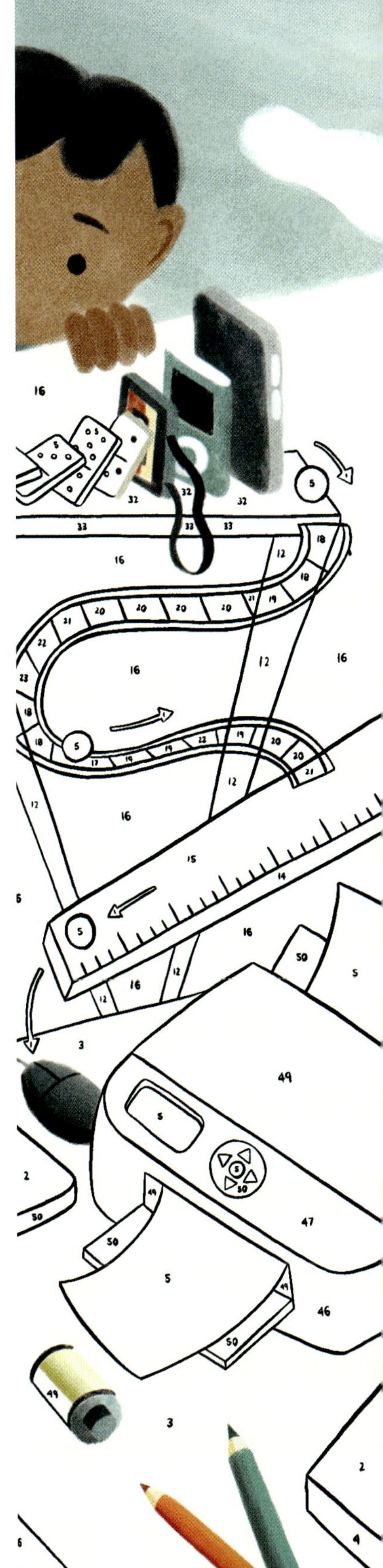

designers working on fiction, poetry, nonfiction and journalistic books. Visual artists who work with paper carefully select the best type, weight and size for their project. As a writer, I spend hours at my local stationery store checking out new styles, shapes and sizes of notebooks. And now that I have taken up collage making, every piece of paper I lay my hands on has potential for my artwork.

When I was a kid, my brother, sister and I listened over and over to a skit about a man who claimed to have invented waterproof cardboard. It seemed like such a wild and improbable idea that it had us in stitches. Think about this next time you get a takeaway drink. New materials, types of source materials, machinery and processes allow us to come up with paper for many purposes and tastes. And paper remains one of the most basic materials used for creative activities and projects.

This fearsome gorilla made of cardboard is by Canadian artist Laurence Vallières.

MEUNIERD/DREAMSTIME.COM

THE ARTS AND CRAFTS MOVEMENT

For centuries, much of what people made—pottery, furniture, cloth, tools—was for their own use at home, on their farms or in their workplaces. Eventually candlemakers, potters, weavers and woodworkers found that they could sell their pots, shawls and chairs to their neighbors and at local markets.

During the Industrial Revolution, from about 1760 to 1820, machines were invented to make many of the things individual craftspeople had been making by hand. Eventually mills produced cloth and paper. Potteries turned out bowls and jugs. Steel factories turned out household items and farm implements. And factories made furniture.

In England, the Arts and Crafts movement of the 1880s was a reaction to the sameness of things created through ***mass production***. The movement believed that something useful could also be beautiful. Individual artists, potters, glassmakers, ceramicists, carpenters, fabric designers, architects and designers brought their own skills and creative vision to making products that continue to be much admired—and used—today. But this movement did not last long, partly because not everyone could afford such finely crafted handmade items. So the manufacturing industry and mass production have continued to be important.

Today the Buy Local movement promotes what we produce closer to home. Buying local means supporting creative people who make beautiful and useful things in our own communities. And it helps reduce the environmental impact of shipping goods long distances.

After the Industrial Revolution, factories like this cloth mill of the early 1900s manufactured items that most people could afford.

EVERETT COLLECTION/SHUTTERSTOCK.COM

THE CHANGING WAYS WE MAKE AND CREATE

Many of the tools we've invented in the past hundred years allow us to create things ourselves, at home and at school, and then share them widely with total strangers as well as people we know. Immersive technology exhibits help us feel as if we're moving through artists' paintings rather than just looking in from the outside. Multilingual robots help visitors navigate museums, galleries and archaeological sites so they get the most out of the experience.

The modern manual potter's wheel is not much different than those that were first used 5,000 years ago.

ATHIMA TONGLOOM/GETTY IMAGES

MAKING MAGIC AT THE MOVIES

When you watch your favorite animated show, you might not guess that the earliest form of animation came in the form of pictures on a Greek vase. As it was rotated, the image changed and shifted as if it were animated. Here's a brief account of how we got to where we are today.

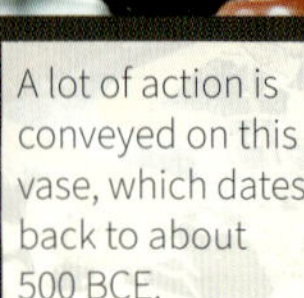

A lot of action is conveyed on this vase, which dates back to about 500 BCE.

ARCHAIOPTIX/ WIKIMEDIA COMMONS/ CC BY-SA 4.0

1600s: The magic lantern used a mirror in the back of a light source (originally a candle) to direct light through long glass slides with images on them. As the slides were fed through the lantern, they created the appearance of movement and are considered the first examples of moving pictures.

1800s: The thaumatrope was an optical toy consisting of a picture disk held by two strings. When the strings are spun to twirl the disk, the image on each side of the disk merges into one, tricking the eye into seeing movement long after the device has stopped spinning.

1900: The silent film *The Enchanted Drawing* contained the first animated sequences recorded on standard picture film.

1908: *Fantasmagorie* was a two-minute stick-figure animation by French cartoonist Émile Cohl. You can find it on YouTube.

1928: Disney's short film *Steamboat Willie* was one of the first animated cartoons to have sound synchronized with its visuals.

1937: *Snow White and the Seven Dwarfs* was Walt Disney's first full-length animated movie. He used cel animation, a process in which objects or characters are hand-drawn on transparent celluloid sheets, placed over painted backgrounds, then filmed in sequence.

1958: Alfred Hitchcock's classic movie *Vertigo* was the first live-action movie to use computer-generated imagery in its opening sequences.

1960s: This is considered the beginning of the era of computer-generated graphics and animation. The field continued to expand and change, with new techniques and technology being developed and used all the time.

2021: *Encanto* made the most money of any animated movie that year. It employed more than 800 people in its production, 108 of whom were animators.

HOME ENTERTAINMENT

The earliest form of home entertainment involved families and community members gathering around the fire to share songs, stories and poetry. If they had musical instruments, they made music together. Later, if the family could afford books, they read to themselves or each other.

Gramophones (later called record players), invented in 1887, allowed people to play music at home on vinyl records.

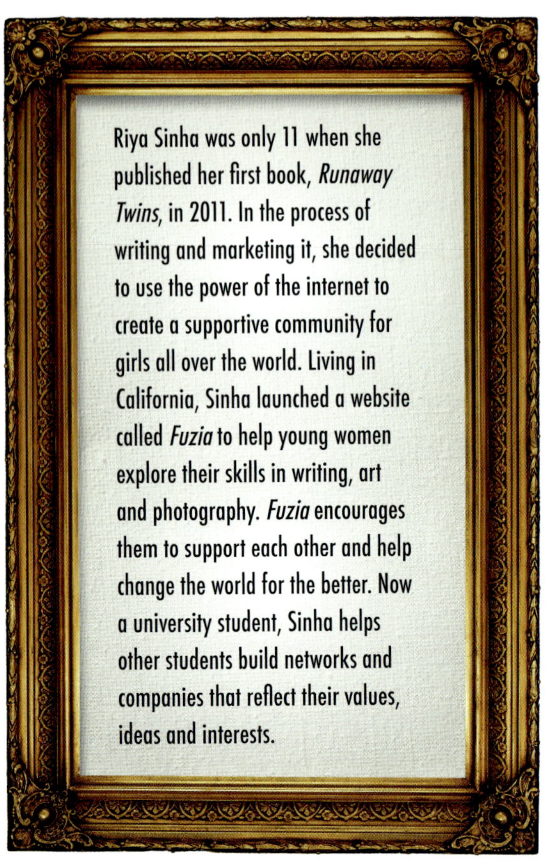

Riya Sinha
Entrepreneur

Originally used for communication between ships and people onshore, radios were introduced into private homes about 10 years later. These brought other voices, stories and music into private homes with the turn of a dial.

When black-and-white TV was introduced in the 1950s, sets were so small that viewers had to sit close to them. TV sets gradually got bigger and the picture got clearer as the technology improved. Color TVs came into use in about 1960. Most early TV viewers had to get up from the couch to turn it on or change the channel until remote controls were invented. These days your TV likely has a bigger, flat screen, surround sound and high-definition pictures. And you get to enjoy streamed music, movies, videos and podcasts.

As home entertainment grows, many writers, editors, directors, set and sound designers, actors, musicians and composers find more outlets for their creative activities. Many people feared that new technology would lead to the death of cinemas and live performances. But although most people have some kind of entertainment system in their own home, movie theaters and concert halls still attract audiences to live music, drama, dance and documentary shows. For example, the MGM Sphere, a music and entertainment arena in Las Vegas, takes IMAX-type productions to new heights. As humans, we will always be looking for new ways to entertain ourselves and each other. And technology will always have a big role to play.

WILD AND WACKY TOOLS AND TECHNOLOGY

British humorist Heath "The Gadget King" Robinson started out as a landscape painter in the late 1880s but soon turned to illustrating books and magazines. He is now best known for his drawings of wild and wacky inventions. Not many look like they would work. But you have to admire his creativity and imaginative thinking. In the United States, Rube Goldberg started doing newspaper comics in 1908. He became famous for his "invention drawings," which depicted complicated chain-reaction machines doing practical tasks in unlikely and highly improbable ways. Since 2001 the Chain Reaction Contraption Contest, whose main sponsor is the Westinghouse Electric company, has set a different Rube Goldberg-like challenge each year. These have included contraptions for transporting an object, wrapping and unwrapping a present and putting toothpaste on a toothbrush.

Not all inventions are practical. Some merely exhibit the makers' creative and innovative minds.

JEFFREY COOLIDGE/GETTY IMAGES

A GOOD LAUGH

Comedy and laughter are important to our society and to everyone's mental health. A Nielsen survey found that people in the United States watched 1.3 trillion minutes of comedy programs on national TV in 2020, during the first year of the COVID-19 pandemic. My dad once had to stop the car because he was laughing so hard at a 1960s radio show called *Beyond the Fringe.* Your family might watch *Home Alone* every year. You might laugh your way through all of Dan Gutman's books. Or be hooked on Mr. Bean reruns or wacky cartoons. Someone in your family may watch YouTubers Rhett and Link, or the Onyx Family TikTok videos. Or share their favorite joke book over dinner. Thankfully, there are always lots of ways for creative people to tickle our funny bones and many ways to get a good laugh.

chapter five

WHERE IN THE WORLD?

In Mexico the Day of the Dead is traditionally celebrated on November 1–2. Families gather for picnics and community events—often in cemeteries—to celebrate their ancestors. Adults and children dress in costume and join colorful parades that fill the streets. And those with a sweet tooth buy colorfully decorated candy skulls. People in different cultures and places engage in creative activities that reflect their values, environment and traditions.

HERE, THERE AND EVERYWHERE

All around the world, distinctive creative activities and traditions are based on a region's environment, weather, history, religion, language and natural materials. Some depend on the human history of the area. For example, Turkey's music, art and architecture reflect its history of invasion and colonization by Greek, Armenian, Arabic, Persian, Balkan and Middle Eastern peoples.

Mexican people have different attitudes about death than people in some other countries. They celebrate the Day of the Dead to remember ancestors and celebrate family and community.
FG TRADE LATIN/GETTY IMAGES

During the Hindu festival of Holi—which celebrates color, spring and love—colored powder is thrown about during boisterous street events.
GRAPHIXEL/GETTY IMAGES

In contrast, the people of North Sentinel Island in the Bay of Bengal have had little contact with outsiders. So their traditions, arts and crafts are likely to be unique to them, as they have not yet been affected or influenced by people outside their culture.

EXPRESSING OUR CULTURES IN CREATIVE WAYS

To the Maori people of New Zealand, the head is the most sacred part of the body. Mataora tattoos on men's faces symbolize nobility. Moko kauae tattoos on women's lips and chins represent leadership and status.

The people of Latacunga, Ecuador, celebrate the Mama Negra festival with music and fireworks. These rituals reflect the region's relationship with the nearby Cotopaxi volcano.

Fireworks have long been used in many countries and cultures to celebrate special traditions and holidays.
HANNAH HAWKINS/GETTY IMAGES

Explorer Marco Polo brought piñatas to Mexico after seeing clay farm animals filled with seeds or small trinkets in Spain, rather than the candy-filled papier-mâché ones we're familiar with today.

The Nuu-chah-nulth First Nations, who live on the northwest coast of North America, and the Mande women in Sierra Leone are two examples of peoples who use masks in cultural ceremonies.

Children in England dress up a "Guy" in old clothes as a way to collect money to buy fireworks for Bonfire Night. This annual November 5 event celebrates Guy Fawkes's unsuccessful attempt to blow up London's Houses of Parliament in 1605. The "Guy" is placed on top of the bonfire as the highlight of the evening's fireworks display.

Yodeling is used in Switzerland to call in farmers' flocks from the mountains and valleys, and to communicate between villages.

Pavlova, my favorite dessert of berries, cream and meringue, was introduced to Australia by the ballet dancer Anna Pavlova. There's a story that another version called Eton Mess was "invented" when someone dropped an entire pavlova during a cricket match at Britain's Eton College.

Shadow puppetry is one of the oldest forms of storytelling. It originates in China. Usually conveying stories from mythology and history, it is popular in Indonesia and Thailand.

The delicate ornamentation on these pysanky is created using a special stylus, powdered dyes and beeswax.
MARSHA SKRYPUCH

Known mainly for her children's books about wartime Europe, author Marsha Forchuk Skrypuch also makes meticulously painted Ukrainian Easter eggs called ***pysanky***, which symbolize the rebirth of the earth at Easter.

The Hwulmuhw people have been knitting with wool from mountain goats and Salish woolly dogs for many generations. Named after their ancestral region of Vancouver Island, Cowichan sweaters are popular for their warmth and water-repellent nature.

Call-and-response singing by South Africa's Zulu and Xhosa people shares news and celebrates community.

The didgeridoo is a wind instrument developed by the Indigenous people of Northern Australia over 1,000 years ago.

Composer Antonín Dvořák wrote the New World Symphony to celebrate his home country of Czechoslovakia when he settled in the United States.

KIDS, CULTURE AND CREATIVITY

The games you play and the creative things you do help you explore and develop a sense of your own culture and identity. In 2022 Andrea Li and Michelle Lim started Toys Aren't Us. Its aim was to create toys that reflected the diverse lives of the kids who played with them and reinforced their cultures. They created a kitchen set that included a grandmother doll to reflect the important role that grandmothers play in

Asian family life. And they renamed some crayon colors Jade, Lemon Tea and Rabbit Candy.

REPRESENTING DIFFERENCES

The US Cooperative Children's Book Center publishes annual statistics of books by authors or with characters who are Black, Indigenous or people of color (BIPOC). In 2022, 40 percent of books the organization received were by people who identify as Black, Indigenous or other people of color. That being said, the number of diverse authors, illustrators and editors has been growing since studies

THE LIFE OF A TOTEM POLE—FROM THE EARTH AND RETURNING TO IT

In a park near where I live, five or six totem poles decompose in the forest. Although there are no signs asking visitors not to move or climb on them, most people are respectful when they come across them, taking away only photos and memories.

The poles were designed, carved and erected by the Snuneymuxw First Nation to celebrate their culture, traditions and mythology, recognize their ancestors and express pride in their community. Usually made from local cedar, a pole includes characteristics specific to the family, community or First Nation it represents. Each pole is carved for its own reason, and there are many different pole types, such as mortuary poles and house front poles. It can take carvers many months to design and carve a pole. The artists who make them are deeply respected and celebrated in their communities, and carving is often a skill passed down in one family.

Raising a new pole is a community event that everyone celebrates. Whether they stand alone in a prominent place in the village or are incorporated into longhouses or other buildings, poles speak of pride in history and tradition and celebrate the creativity and skills of the people who carve them. Once they are no longer strong enough to serve their original purpose, the poles may be laid back in the forest where they came from.

Totem poles laid to rest in a park in Nanaimo, BC, reflect the area's Indigenous culture and history.

LOIS PETERSON

LOGOS

Wherever things are bought and sold or advertised, logos are one way we recognize them, whether they're on a car, pair of runners, computer, construction toy or delivery van. Logos are the creative work of people who not only understand art and design but also have insights into how to attract people's attention. We may be exposed to more than 5,000 logos a day, whether we notice them or not.

The most famous logo was invented by Coca-Cola's bookkeeper, Frank M. Robinson. In 1886 he suggested that "the two Cs would look well in advertising." He then designed the image himself. The color and background of the logo has changed, but the basic design is still recognizable all over the world. Ninety-four percent of the world's population recognizes the logo. This could account for the 1.9 million bottles and cans of Coca-Cola sold worldwide every day.

began in 1985. The number of books the center received that were by BIPOC or about BIPOC characters tripled between 2015 and 2020.

As a society, we acknowledge that in the past the creative work, voices and experiences of other cultures and people have too often been adopted and adapted by people without direct knowledge. In many cases the representations did not reflect the original culture or situation in authentic or respectful ways.

Clothing and jewelry with Indigenous designs have been manufactured and sold by non-Indigenous people. Books featuring LGBTQ+ main characters have been written by authors with no direct or personal experience. Religious artifacts, such as statues of the Buddha, have been used in nonreligious ways. This use of something without the right or permission to use it is called cultural appropriation.

Readers, audiences and shoppers deserve to see, read, hear and buy creative work that authentically conveys their own culture, gender, language and personal experience. And writers, artists and filmmakers need to be able to represent their own experiences freely so that we can understand and appreciate the great diversity of humanity, the world and our creative efforts.

CREATIVITY AND RELIGION

At my school in England, my classmates and I attended weekly Sunday services at Truro Cathedral. I was often distracted by the sun shining through the stained-glass windows, the music pouring from the organ loft overhead, and the carvings on the stone pillars and archways.

For centuries, all over the world, craftspeople and artists have contributed to religious and spiritual life. Architects, builders, stonemasons and carvers created many of the spaces in which we worship, including churches, mosques and temples. Musicians, writers, poets, singers, actors,

dancers and composers have brought religious stories to life for congregations, services and prayers. Stained-glass designers, candlemakers, painters, tile-makers, carvers and fabric artists have created beautiful things we use or see around us when we gather to worship. Calligraphers have recorded religious teachings, stories and mythology in religious documents. And many people have written fiction and nonfiction books about faith and spiritual belief.

Whether we practice one of the more than 4,000 religious faiths in the world or are nonreligious, we encounter creative work celebrating religious life and faith wherever we are in the world.

RELIGIOUS PERFORMANCES

People come from all over the world to watch a ***passion play*** in the small German town of Oberammergau. It tells the story of Jesus's work, life, trial and death and has been performed on open-air stages every 10 years since 1634 to commemorate the community's survival after the bubonic plague swept through the town. Today more than 2,000 actors, musicians and production people are involved in putting on the performance—all from the local village.

In Turkey some Muslim men are practicing Sufis who perform activities they believe bring them closer to God. One activity is a ritual dance that dates back to the 13th century, when mystic and poet Rumi promoted dance as a form of meditation.

Orhan Pamuk
Author

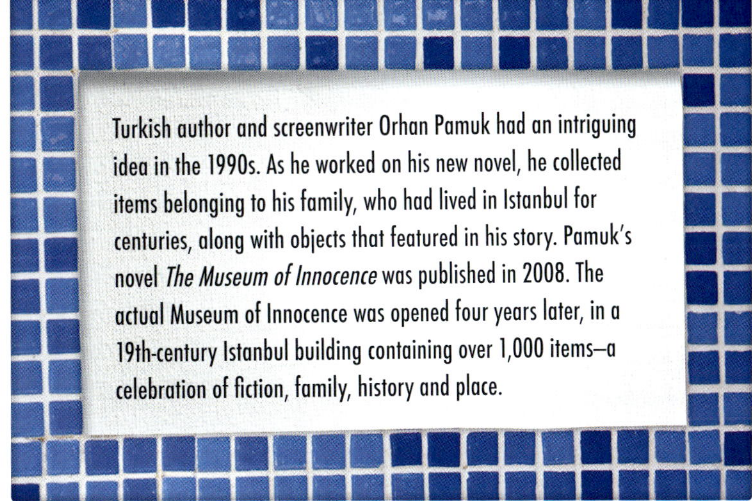

The dance is known for its mesmerizing movements and haunting music, and the dancers are known as whirling dervishes. During the dance, the palm of one of the dancer's hands faces the sky while the other hand faces the earth to represent the connection of earth to heaven. Dervishes wear black or brown conical hats to represent tombstones, depicting the death of their own sense of self-importance. Banned for many years by the government, whirling dervishes most often perform for tourists. But the ritual dance is still conducted in dervish lodges and hermitages and other religious sites throughout Turkey.

chapter six

THE WAY WE SEE IT

Early art could only show humans accurately from the outside, as so little was known about anatomy. But many artists took some wild guesses about what our innards might have looked like! In the medieval era, people who had never seen an elephant, sloth or oyster conveyed animals and other creatures in creative and imaginative ways, which were often far from natural or realistic. As time passes and we change, so do the knowledge, ideas and values we express, the skills we use to convey them and the tools we use and how we use them.

How we convey the world around us is based on our experience, knowledge and imagination.
WIKIMEDIA COMMONS/PUBLIC DOMAIN

GENDER

Bias against women has long been present all over the world, in daily life, business, politics and the creative world. Men performed all the female roles in plays from the time of the ancient Greeks up until the 17th century. Two female artists who were founding members of the Royal Academy of Arts in London in 1768 were not allowed to participate as fully as male members. Nineteenth-century French author Amantine Lucile Aurore Dupin used the pen name George Sand in order to get published.

In many creative fields, women's work is still not recognized and valued in the same way as men's. There continues to be a big difference between what men and women are paid and what creative opportunities are open to them. Women haven't always been represented in art, plays and movies in authentic and realistic ways. A US organization called the National Museum of Women in the Arts studies gender differences that still exist in many creative disciplines.

DIVERSITY ON STAGE AND SCREEN

Until relatively recently, not many roles that conveyed people with disabilities were played by actors who themselves lived with the condition. And it was hard for performers who lived with disabilities to find work on the stage or screen. Today creative people from all backgrounds have many more opportunities to publish their writing, show their art, record their music, lead orchestras and act and direct in movies.

Mila Davis-Kent is a deaf Black actor. She was only 10 when she played the role of Amara in the box office hit *Creed III*. The TV series *The Healing Power of Dudes* features a young man with an anxiety disorder, based on the writer's own experience. His on-screen friend—someone with cerebral palsy—is played by an actor with cerebral palsy. And actor Michael J. Fox continued to act long after he began to be affected by Parkinson's disease.

With many people pushing for inclusive roles for everyone, we are a little closer to portraying the full range of human experience on paper, screen, stage and canvas. Viewers, readers and audiences have more opportunities to participate in and share creative work, and to see themselves authentically represented in creative projects. For a richer, more inclusive world, changes in attitude are not enough. We also need tools and equipment that allow everyone to participate in a creative life, whether that means watching, reading, exploring or making.

BLACKFACE

The first time I saw the 1965 movie of Shakespeare's play *Othello*, the white actor playing the part of Othello—a Black man—wore so much dark makeup that I expected it to melt in the heat of the film-set lights. That same night, my grandmother might have been watching *The Black and White Minstrel Show*. This English TV program ran for 20 years. It featured white singers performing songs from the American south in blackface—dark makeup used by white people in order to mock Black people. The *Minstrel* program has been described as "the BBC's most glaring failure to understand the damage it could do when it traded in outdated ***stereotypes***." At about the same time, Black performers in the United States were still forbidden from performing in many southern states. Thankfully, in most places we now have different ideas about conveying people of other races and genders in appropriate and respectful ways.

MORE THAN A HELPING HAND

Following are adaptive and assistive technologies that help people with physical challenges function in creative, work and educational environments:

Voice-to-text software allows writers with poor vision to dictate their work into a computer, which ***transcribes*** it and reads it back to them.

A recently developed computer mouse can be controlled by blowing through a straw.

A pair of glasses allows the user to control their computer cursor by moving their head.

Photographers who have limited use of their fingers or hands can operate the shutter release by biting down on a special switch.

Easy-to-grip brushes and other devices help artists and sculptors control the tools they need for their creative work.

Digital instruments and keyboards help musicians create and make music even if they cannot manipulate a guitar, violin, drum, piano, etc.

Sensory-friendly programs in theaters allow neuro-diverse people to watch a show comfortably.

Advanced recording devices help actors and performers who are affected with dyslexia and other reading challenges learn and memorize scripts.

Special wheelchairs enable dancers to move around and interact with other dancers.

More and more venues include accessibility features that help people make their way inside and be comfortable while they listen to music, watch a play or see an art exhibit.

New technology is being invented all the time. Some tools are created by people like Brenda Chapman (see sidebar), who need it themselves. Others are invented by specialists who want everyone to have access to whatever they need to pursue their goals and interests.

Bridges Canada collects information and distributes assistive technology tools that are created worldwide. And it gives schools and colleges the opportunity to test-drive new equipment that helps their students. In the United States, the Center on Technology and Disability conducts research on new tools that help students and teachers.

Brenda Chapman
Writer and Painter

Brenda Chapman has written more than 20 adult mystery novels and is also a painter. She has faced various physical challenges in her life, including tremors, which these days make it hard for her to sign her name.

When a pinched nerve in her neck affected her right hand and arm, she went looking for tools to help. Working with the Neil Squire Society, she helped develop equipment to aid other writers and artists, such as a paint-tube holder that makes handling the tube easier. This was so popular that even members of Chapman's art group who did not have similar physical challenges wanted one too. "I think we are only limited by our imagination," says Chapman. "I am going to turn it into a game, to see what other things I can come up with that need fixing."

FAMOUS PEOPLE PLAYERS

In 1974 three organizers brought together 11 puppeteers to perform a black-light show called *Aruba Liberace*. It included a life-sized puppet of world-famous musician Liberace playing the piano. Liberace himself was so impressed that he invited the company to appear onstage with him in Las Vegas.

Black-light puppetry is performed in the dark on a stage lit by ultraviolet lighting. The puppeteers are almost invisible—they dress in black and manipulate bright-colored puppets against a black background. The Famous People Players now travel the world and have more than 30 different shows. Every performer in the company lives with a physical or intellectual disability. The company that began with just three people managing and booking shows, making costumes and writing scripts for 11 performers now performs for large audiences of puppetry lovers and theatergoers worldwide.

THE THREE RS OF CREATIVITY

Every day it becomes even more important to take care of our planet as we witness the effects of the climate crisis on the environment. Try to incorporate the principles of reduce, recycle and reuse into your own creative activities.

When you gather scrap paper for a collage, cut up old T-shirts to braid into wristbands or rugs, or convert plastic milk bottles into snow globes, you are not only being a good steward of the earth's resources but are also pushing the boundaries of creativity.

Rather than leaving discarded materials to contaminate the ground, Michael Dudley, the Barefooted Welder in Australia, makes spectacular sculptures from discarded steel, metal and copper. In San Francisco, Erika Iris Simmons creates portraits of musicians using old cassette and VHS tapes. In 2016 artist Tan Zi Xi exhibited her large-scale art installation *Plastic Ocean* at the Singapore Art Museum. The installation uses more than 20,000 pieces of plastic collected from the ocean to give gallery visitors the feeling of what it might be like to drown in plastic trash.

Tie-dyeing is a colorful way to upcycle old T-shirts.
SIX_CHARACTERS/GETTY IMAGES

CLOSER TO HOME

According to one survey, only about 20 percent of Americans upcycle clothing, boxes and other goods. But in many homes, old furniture does get repaired or altered instead of being

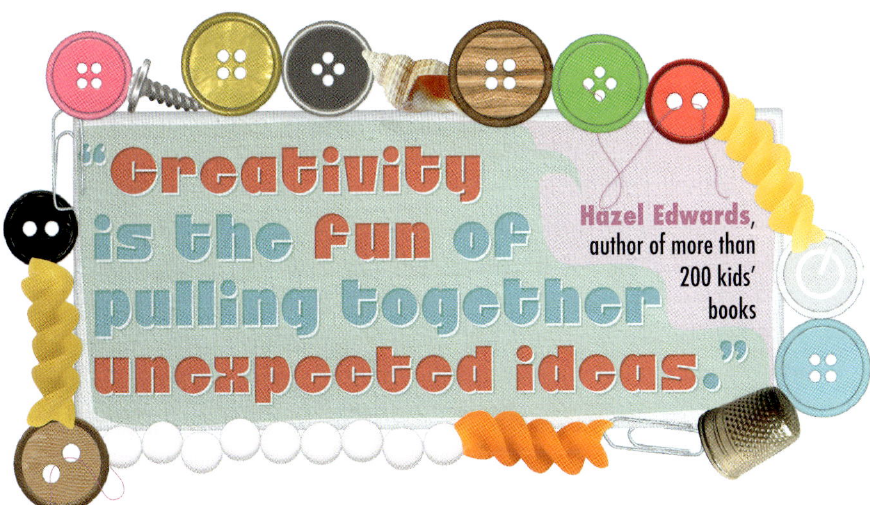

thrown in the garbage. Vintage tablecloths, pillowcases and curtains get new life as clothing. Old tins get freshened up with paint and collage and are used for storing paintbrushes, buttons or shells. Old jewelry is assembled into pictures and collages. Timber from old barns and houses is used to make furniture.

Following the three Rs means using only what we need, finding new uses for things that might otherwise end up in the landfill and considering the source of materials and tools—how they are made and shipped. It involves educating ourselves about ecologically damaging ingredients that might be in paint, solvents, glues and paper. The *Upcycle That* website offers ideas about what to do with hundreds of products, including fabric, wood and wax.

RECYCLED ORCHESTRA OF CATEURA

Many musicians performing in concert halls all around the world play beautiful handcrafted instruments. In Paraguay local ***entrepreneur*** and ***philanthropist*** Favio Chavez wanted children living in Cateura, a huge slum alongside a landfill near Asunción, to have a chance to make music.

Members of the Recycled Orchestra of Cateura show off their locally made instruments and musical skills with pride.
WENN RIGHTS LTD/ALAMY STOCK PHOTO

But he could not find enough instruments for everyone who wanted to learn. So he challenged local carpenter Nicolas Gomez to recycle some of Cateura's garbage into musical instruments.

Although Cola, as Gomez is known, had no musical experience, he came through. He made stringed, wind and percussion instruments from metal, cardboard and paper found at the dump. Dozens of kids signed up for lessons, and eventually they formed the Recycled Orchestra of Cateura. In the years since, many kids from Cateura have performed for music lovers all over the world on their locally made instruments.

NEW LIFE FOR OLD MATERIALS

One evening I visited a place on Vancouver Island where night fishers sit in their lantern-lit boats on the dark water. It was a magical sight. But even more magical was the creature that seemed ready to leap out of the nearby bushes. It was a coyote, made entirely out of driftwood. It seemed so alive, I have never forgotten the moment I first glimpsed it.

We are constantly seeking different ways to use and reuse natural materials, thereby wasting fewer valuable resources. Concern for the future of our world and environment is so great that it drives many creative people's choice of what they do, make and create and how they do it.

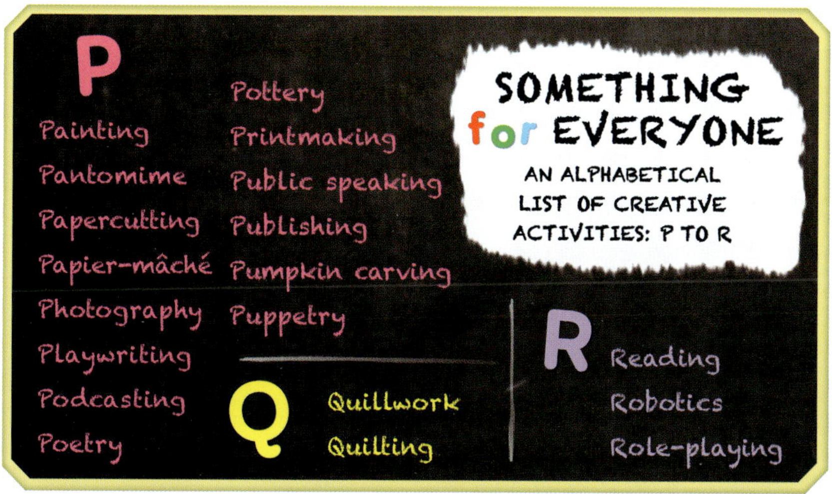

chapter seven

CHANGING OURSELVES AND OUR WORLD

The Breadwinner series, written by Canadian author Deborah Ellis, examine the plight of women and girls in Afghanistan. Chinese artist Ai Weiwei created an exhibit of 2,000 life jackets to bring attention to the 2,000 refugees who died at sea while trying to escape from repression and persecution in Syria. The big topics that affect us and our world are reflected as much in art, writing, music, movies and plays as they are in news reports.

Creative expression that conveys concern for the world and environment encourages us all to learn more and come up with solutions.

ALISTAIR BERG/GETTY IMAGES

NEVER TOO YOUNG

In 2022 three New Jersey teens, Vivian Xie, Anushri Dwivedi and Rachael Kapoor, won the year's Bow Seat Ocean Awareness Contest for their film *Bergaville*. Available on YouTube, it's their quirky take on the causes of rising sea levels. They wanted to inform people about the consequences of climate change in a way that was not too harsh or judgmental and that would encourage viewers to take action.

Every two years the Massachusetts-based Bow Seat Ocean Awareness Programs invite 11- to 18-year-old students from all over the world to submit work—creative writing, visual art, poetry and spoken word, film, performing arts, or interactive or media presentations—that explores their relationships to the changing world and encourages positive change.

Each of us is changed when we do creative work—whether it's making a movie, reading or making up a story, painting a picture, dancing, composing a song, acting in a play or choosing flowers for a bouquet. And that work gives audiences, viewers and participants a chance to look at themselves and their world differently. Art, music, dance, theater, architecture and design all have the potential to change the world we live in. Many of our problems can be addressed through creativity and innovation.

Arts and crafts helped injured soldiers of World War I regain their physical and mental health and also deal with the trauma of their experiences.

OTIS HISTORICAL ARCHIVES, NATIONAL MUSEUM OF HEALTH & MEDICINE/ WIKIMEDIA COMMONS/CC BY-SA 2.0

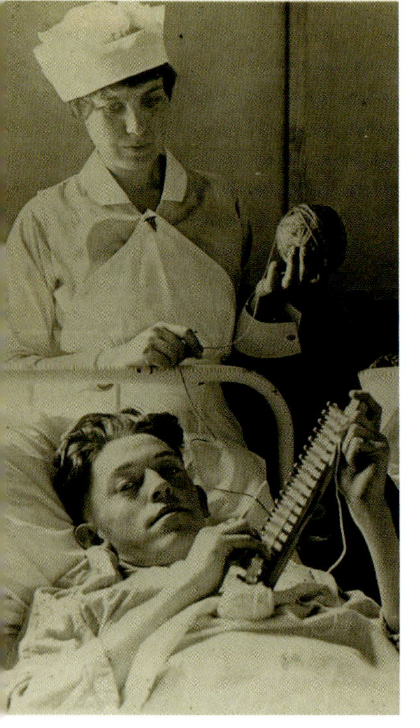

OCCUPATIONAL THERAPY

Occupational therapy (OT) was first offered in 1917 to provide meaningful activities for injured soldiers, airmen and sailors returning from World War I. The first activity provided was basket weaving, which enabled the patients to produce something useful while they were healing.

In Canada the Red Cross established Vetcraft shops. Here the public could buy various items created by wounded veterans, and salesmen traveled the country selling their work. Sales of Vetcraft work dropped in the 1930s, but OT continued to help wounded, injured and ill people regain and develop physical function and skills and find a creative outlet.

Occupational therapy became a profession that many creative people took up to help other people live more productive and meaningful lives. In Canada there are more than 20,000 occupational therapists. In the United States, 131,000 OTs work in hospitals, care homes, recreational facilities and patients' homes.

HELPING AND HEALING

I recently gave away an easel to a teenager who was finding 10th grade really stressful. Coming home every day to do a little bit of art really helps her. People who have experienced physical or mental trauma or challenges can benefit from many kinds of creative expression.

A famous painting is *The Starry Night* by Vincent van Gogh. Although he is perhaps best known for cutting off his own ear during a ***psychotic*** episode, he had long creative periods when his mental health was stable. During this time he created great masterpieces of ***Impressionistic art***.

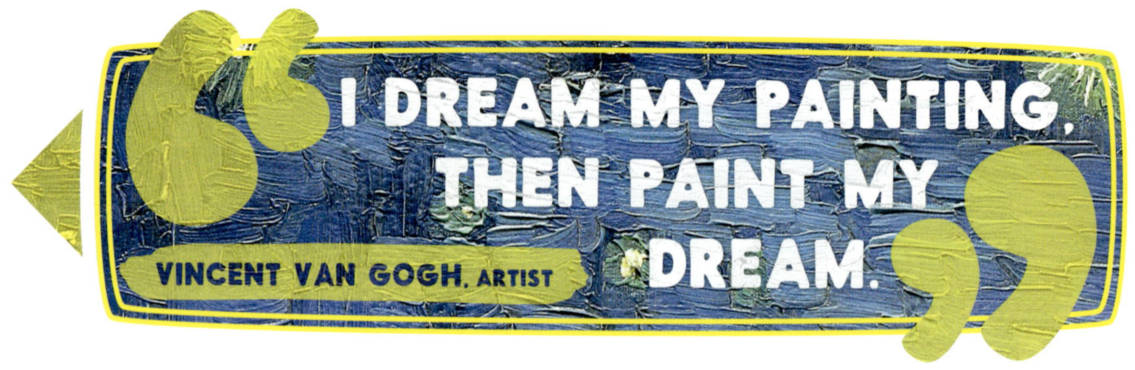

But even when he was struggling, he was able to be productive, using his art to express his personal life and situation.

Illness, injury and trauma are often evident on our physical bodies. Healing what has damaged us mentally can take a long time.

BENJAVISA RUANGVAREE ART/ SHUTTERSTOCK.COM

THE RESILIENCE ART PROJECT

After a mass shooting in El Paso, Texas, in 2019, the community looked for ways to develop ***resilience*** and help local people heal from the trauma and pain of the incident. Working with an organization called Creative Kids, and with funds from the state, the Resilience Art Project was born. It offered workshops, panel discussions and exhibits to encourage people to express their feelings in creative ways as a way to recover from what they had been through. A year later, adults and children who had used their creativity to help them process their feelings exhibited their art, poetry and collages in a show called *El Paso, Even Stronger.*

THE HURT INSIDE

If you are having a hard time with identity, bullying or any other personal or family challenge, you may find that doing something creative helps you process experiences and feelings. Writing, art, music, sculpture or dancing help many people find acceptance and recognition without the need to publicly share information about their personal lives and struggles.

In 2014 the filmmaker Lee Hirsch, director of the 2011 documentary film *Bully*, created the digital Bully Project Mural. Its 16 art panels reflected people's attitudes toward and experiences of bullying. The mural later expanded to include artists from around the world, who contributed paintings, graphics, collages and prints of their own.

Remember Arthur Lobel's heartwarming Frog and Toad stories? Many are about friendship and caring and respecting one another. Lobel said he used his own childhood experiences and emotions to help young readers explore theirs.

PROSTHETICS: FROM WOODEN TOES TO MICROCHIP-CONTROLLED LIMBS

Creativity plays an important role in how we solve problems and address challenges. The innovative thinking that scientists, inventors and other creative people use to find ways to replace lost or damaged limbs makes a huge difference to many people's lives.

More than 3,000 years ago, an unnamed Egyptian noblewoman may have been the first person to use a prosthetic device. Whether she was born without a big toe or lost it in an accident, we don't know. But the wooden and leather toe created for her must have allowed her greater mobility.

Improvements in methods of amputation in the 1500s led to the use of wood and leather prosthetic arms and legs, attached with leather straps and buckles. Later, doctors working with people wounded in wartime helped develop early versions of the prostheses used today for adults and children. New materials and construction methods create lighter, more manageable replacement legs, arms and hands. Digital technology allows for microchip-controlled limbs, and carbon fiber is used in flexible prostheses that allow runners to compete against athletes who have full use of their legs and arms.

THE POWER OF MUSIC

In a drum circle, people gather to make music with drums and other percussion instruments. The circle allows people to express themselves through rhythm and connect with others in the group. The energy of the circle can be uplifting and energizing. And drumming does not require words or even eye contact.

Scientists studying mental health and brain activity have discovered that making music or watching it being performed can improve a person's mood, cheering them up

when they are feeling low and calming them when they feel agitated. Some people take up an instrument for the first time as a way to deal with mental-health issues.

Music can help activate the part of the brain associated with memory for people suffering from Alzheimer's disease or dementia. These conditions affect what they remember and who they recognize. If they listen to familiar music, they can often reconnect for a while with their past and the people in their lives, and they may also find it calming if they are feeling anxious.

DEAR DIARY

Early on in my six years at boarding school, I had a journal with a gray leather cover and a tiny page for each day. Every night I wrote about what I had done, what had happened in school that day and how I was feeling. I sketched things and people around me. I created fictional characters and wrote their life stories—my version of imaginary friends. I could express what I felt, surrounded by more than 40 other girls, many teachers and house matrons. It was my safe place in a rather confusing world.

Whether this teen keeps her diary to herself or shares it with others, she can use it to explore her feelings and the world around her.

RYAN MCVAY/GETTY IMAGES

Journaling can be a great way to explore feelings, experiences and creative ideas. You don't need to worry about spelling and grammar—you can just can express yourself in any way that feels comfortable. You only need a notebook and pen, a computer or other digital device. A few minutes here, a few more there. For some people, writing in a journal helps them develop skills they can apply to poetry, stories, comics or song lyrics. Or they may use their journal to reflect their world by sketching what they see around them.

Anne Frank wrote a diary when her family was in hiding from the Nazis during World War II. When the diary was published as *The Diary of a Young Girl*, it sold more than 30 million copies in 70 languages. Journals like hers help people in dangerous and difficult times and situations process feelings and experiences. Their writing can also provide a record of an important time, helping readers understand historical events.

North America has a long tradition of musicians using songs to comment on their lives and times. In 2015 Environment Canada scientist and folk singer Tony Turner wrote and performed "Harperman." His song was a commentary on the policies of then prime minister Stephen Harper and the Conservative government in power at the time. But his song got Turner suspended from his job for contravening his department's values and ethics code by criticizing the government.

Turner's union helped him fight to keep his job and prove his right to sing the song, based in large part on a 1991 Supreme Court ruling that found that, with only a few exceptions, public servants are entitled to the same free-speech rights that all Canadian citizens have under the Canadian Charter of Rights and Freedoms. Many other musicians, music lovers, government staff and fans also supported Turner and his music. Due to the stress of the long investigation, Turner finally took early retirement from a job he loved rather than wait out a decision about whether he could keep working for the government.

Tony Turner
Musician

FREEDOM OF EXPRESSION

Your school or public library probably mounts a display each year to promote Freedom to Read Week. Held in the last week of February, it emphasizes everyone's right to read what they want. It encourages readers to pick up books that have been banned in schools, libraries and communities. And the campaign supports the right of authors to write freely on any topic or in any way.

This right to creative expression—called intellectual freedom—is included in the laws that govern what citizens

Standing up for the right to read is something parents, teachers, librarians and readers do to ensure that everyone has access to all kinds of books.

JOHN RAMSPOTT/WIKIMEDIA COMMONS/ CC BY-SA 2.0

and residents are entitled to do. But throughout history and in many parts of the world, creative people and their work have been subjected to ***censorship*** and punishment.

A number of countries' laws limit or prohibit artistic expression, especially if it's seen to criticize the government or legal system. Writers, actors, directors and artists in countries such as Turkey, Russia and China often have to go underground to hide their work and protect themselves from punishment or imprisonment. In countries like Canada and the United States, some people try to prevent movies, art or plays from being seen. Some pressure school boards, individual schools or teachers, ***picket*** libraries, organize protests and generally try to stop kids like you from reading what you like.

THE MCCARTHY ERA

In the United States, a period in the 1950s became known as the McCarthy Era. During this time, writers, artists, actors and filmmakers who were known to support or even just suspected of supporting ***communism*** were ***blacklisted*** by the government. It was a campaign led by Republican Senator Joseph McCarthy. People on the list were not allowed to work in Hollywood, and they could not have their work performed or displayed publicly. Many people's reputations were ruined and it was difficult for them to make a living.

EXPRESS YOURSELF

Protesters' objections to public art, exhibits or shows might be based on community standards—ideas about what some people consider acceptable in a particular region or neighborhood. Or their actions might come from their religious beliefs, personal opinions and preferences. Hundreds of books are banned from the shelves of classrooms and libraries every year.

An organization called PEN International speaks out on behalf of writers, visual artists, journalists, actors and playwrights wherever they are discriminated against or their work is threatened. The American Library Association lists organizations around the world that support the rights of writers, artists and playwrights.

As humans, we need to be able to read and write books, perform and watch plays, take photos, make art, perform dances, write music, sing songs and make statues and carvings about any topic—to reflect what's good about our world and to express what troubles or distresses us and suggest ways to change things.

Even in Canada and the United States, where citizens have some of the strongest protections of intellectual freedom, we still need to ensure that everyone is able to express themselves freely and that we have the right to consume and enjoy all kinds of creative work.

chapter eight

GOOD, BETTER, BEST

"I find a nice thing and take a picture of it and just find a way to make it look nice," said 10-year-old Lilly of Calgary when she participated in the Kids Photography Academy challenges in 2020. Like 160 other children from all over the world, Lilly posted one of her photos online every day for 30 days. Not for recognition. Or for money. But as a way to learn how to do something new.

It may take time to learn to use a camera. But taking photographs will help you see the world in a new way and provide a way to share what you see with others.

POLLYANA VENTURA/GETTY IMAGES

MASTERY: NINE STEPS TO GETTING GOOD AT ALMOST ANYTHING

I often tell my writing students, "The more you write, the easier it gets. The more you write, the better you get." As a beginner sketcher and painter, I am told that by my teachers too. This applies to almost any craft, creative work or skill. Reading about it, watching

Helen Hayes,
Actor

videos or observing others can be helpful and inspiring. But putting your fingers to a keyboard, laying paint on a page, sewing the first seam on a shirt...taking that first shot at something is what gets you started, and it's where the pleasure of discovery lies. Following are the steps for developing great skill at doing anything.

1. **FIND A TEACHER.** Many of us learn better from others than by figuring it out by ourselves. Your teacher might be a how-to book, YouTube video or someone who does what you want to learn to do.

2. **COPY AN EXAMPLE.** Sometimes a valuable way to learn is to copy something you want to make or create.

3. **DO IT A LOT.** Your brain adapts and changes when you practice a new skill. You will get the hang of it if you do it often rather than just once in a while.

4. **ACCEPT YOUR EARLY EFFORTS.** Be curious rather than judging them. Ask yourself, What have I got here? What do I need to do next? How have I surprised myself?

5. **LOOK FOR THE BEST BITS.** By looking for the best parts of what you have just done, you reinforce the idea that yes, you can do this! This is important, even if you still have a way to go to reach your goal.

6. **WORK WITH INTENTION.** Know what you want to achieve *this time*. If you're painting, concentrate on one corner of the picture rather than the whole thing at once. If you're doing papercutting, perhaps test different types of paper before you worry about the overall design.

Working from an online recipe can help you try cooking for your family for the first time.

VISUALSPACE/GETTY IMAGES

7. **KEEP TRYING.** Being a beginner is often a good place to be—you're open to ideas, new techniques and suggestions from others. There's no need to be in a rush to get good at something. If you enjoy the journey, the end product will be even more satisfying.

8. **SHARE WHAT YOU HAVE LEARNED.** This is how creative ideas and work spread from place to place, person to person. And you will gain confidence by the responses you get from others.

9. **CELEBRATE.** At every step of the process, take a moment to recognize how far you have come.

VALUING CREATIVITY

On school visits I am often asked how much money I make. It's understandable. In our society, people are often judged by their financial value as much as by who they are and what they do. How much does the performer make for each video? What did that mansion cost the rapper? Who paid what for the famous pictures sold at auction?

Creativity often arises from people trying what no one has ever done before or doing something familiar in a new way.

AND WHEN IT DOES NOT WORK OUT?

When the artist Vincent van Gogh said, "I am always doing that which I cannot do, in order that I may learn how I may do it," he was talking about intellectual risk-taking. Taking risks—testing new ideas, doing something for the first time—is an important part of creativity. Even if something you did for the first time or did differently than last time does not work out, it helps build your confidence. And you are more likely to take creative risks next time.

The Museum of Failure in Brooklyn, New York, displays more than 150 failed items, such as inflatable furniture that leaked and purple ketchup. Neither were practically or commercially successful, but they do demonstrate the creativity, imagination and resilience of their inventors. One popular exhibit is a wall of sticky notes on which museum-goers write down their own recent failures. As the museum founder, Dr. Samuel West, says, "A failure is when your efforts don't lead to the expected or desired results." But that does not mean you should not try!

It takes courage to admit our failures. But it also gives us a chance to recognize goals and demonstrates a willingness to take risks.
DALE CRUSE/WIKIMEDIA COMMONS/CC BY-SA 2.0

Taking risks. Spending their time in ways that are meaningful and fulfilling to them on a personal level. And we can't always put a price on the things we do, make or experiment with. Our creative efforts don't always lead to money or fame. This might lead you to consider why our society values the work of doctors, property developers and hockey players over janitors and writers. And why some families push their kids into being lawyers or bankers rather than plumbers or musicians.

FOR LOVE OR MONEY

Some artists, batik makers, stained-glass artists and other people doing creative things earn a living from what they love doing. Others, struggling to invent a new tool, write a song or build the world's best tree house, do what they do for the joy of it. If someone wants to pay them for their work, that's just gravy—a bonus on top of the satisfaction of pursuing their creative goals.

Some countries formally support the creative life of their citizens as a way of promoting culture. Arts councils help promote artists and their work and create opportunities for them to learn and share. Governments fund art centers and galleries. They provide grants to publishers, writers, artists, musicians and others to allow them to work on creative projects. Art festivals, theaters, music performances and shows are often supported by public funds that come from taxpayers. Foundations and other charitable organizations raise money to support creativity in their communities.

A few countries, including Slovenia, Finland, Austria and Italy, provide pensions to retired artists and performers. But changing priorities and challenging financial times in many countries often affect governments' ability or desire to support the arts and creativity when people need so many other things.

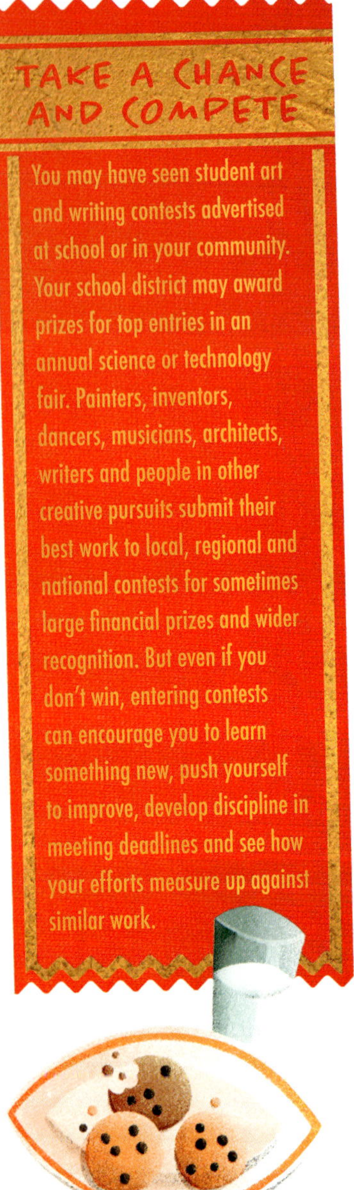

TAKE A CHANCE AND COMPETE

You may have seen student art and writing contests advertised at school or in your community. Your school district may award prizes for top entries in an annual science or technology fair. Painters, inventors, dancers, musicians, architects, writers and people in other creative pursuits submit their best work to local, regional and national contests for sometimes large financial prizes and wider recognition. But even if you don't win, entering contests can encourage you to learn something new, push yourself to improve, develop discipline in meeting deadlines and see how your efforts measure up against similar work.

CREATIVITY AND EDUCATION

A 2019 survey of 500 students found that 71 percent of them wanted careers in the arts. But 43 percent of parents in the survey group wanted their kids to pursue careers in fields such as finance and engineering. The researchers concluded that many adults' hopes for their kids' futures were based on lack of information about career opportunities in various creative fields.

How our society values creativity and imagination is often reflected in our culture, schools and education systems. Many educators bring a creative approach to teaching. But not all children get encouragement for their creativity in school or at home. In some cultures, academic learning is still considered more important than creativity and play.

Your teachers and librarians might encourage your imagination and creativity. Your school might offer art classes or clubs, a drama group, a choir or maker space, or present school concerts, plays or displays of students' artwork.

Some schools focus on creativity and the arts, such as the Langley Fine Arts School in British Columbia, and Walnut Hill School for the Arts in Massachusetts.

BACK TO BASICS

In 2022 researchers at the Bodleian Library, the main research library at Oxford University, UK, studied historical documents in their archives to learn more about who had written them and the times in which those authors had lived. In one 1,300-year-old book they found scribbles and doodles in the margins and between the lines of text.

Today perhaps the most basic and readily available tools and materials for creativity are still paper and pencil.

You can get a message across with paint, markers and special materials—or simply with paper and pencil.

IVETAVAICULE/GETTY IMAGES

Whether you're on a plane, visiting a relative, waiting in a doctor's office or sitting at your kitchen table, you can create something with just those two things. You might use an old envelope, a piece of printer paper, a flyer, a restaurant place mat, the back of last week's math quiz or a grocery bag. You can write, draw, doodle and diagram. You can fold paper into a boat or tear it into the shape of a dragon. You might make up a song. Map out an imaginary world. Plan a tree fort. Design your next Halloween costume. With just these two very basic items, you can be creative in all kinds of ways.

And add just one thing—a glue stick, a colored marker, a pair of scissors, a paper clip—and anything is possible! There's always more to see, learn and do. New ideas to consider. Different ways to approach problems and challenges. There are so many creative ways to express ourselves, to discover and share. And the world is a better place for whatever we do, wherever we do it.

MY CHALLENGE TO YOU

One day on your way to school or gymnastics practice, or on an outing with your parents or caregivers, look around you. Make an inventory

LEE EDWARD FODI

The first time I met Canadian author Lee Edward Födi, he was wandering around a library wearing a wizard's hat, a crowd of kids in tow. Sometimes known as the Wizard of Words or the Daydreaming Doodler, Födi has written seven books and illustrated his own and five others. During school visits and presentations, he engages students with words and stories from the wilds of his imagination. He helps them create fantasy maps, make bejeweled dragon eggs, concoct potions or spells, or weave magic brooms. Lee offers creative possibilities around worldbuilding and storytelling for all the kids he comes into contact with. I am only sorry I did not get to see the worst Christmas tree ornaments that a group of Födi's students came up with in one school presentation.

Lee Edward Födi
Author

of everything you see or hear that reflects creativity—in gardens or store windows, on posters, signs and ads, in the sounds coming from open windows of homes, cars and school classrooms, on the clothing and jewelry of people walking down the street. You might compare notes with others you are with. Recognize and celebrate how everyone—including you—contributes to our world in so many creative ways!

GLOSSARY

anatomy—the study of the structural makeup of people and animals

artifacts—objects made, used or modified by humans that give us information about life in the past

artisans—skilled people who make things with their hands

blacklisted—put on a list of people who are to be punished or excluded

censorship—the practice of suppressing or deleting work that is considered objectionable

choreographed—arranged or made up dance steps and sequences

communism—a political system in which the government controls major resources and wealth is divided among citizens equally or according to individual need

ecological—of or relating to the relationships between living things and their natural environments

entrepreneur—a person who takes charge of creating an activity or business, working as their own employer

fashionista—a designer or follower of the latest fashions

feminist—someone who supports and promotes the political, economic, and social equality of all people regardless of gender

Impressionistic art—a style of art that creates an idea or impression of a subject rather than representing it literally

intellectual—the capacity to reason and work things out

mass production—making a product in large numbers and at a low cost, using specialized equipment and workers

modern art—art that uses techniques and materials in new ways and focuses on subjects not previously used

occupational therapy—treatment that helps people regain everyday functions through practical and creative activities

passion play—a religious drama dealing with Christ's suffering, death and resurrection

philanthropist—someone who provides money or services to benefit others rather than themselves

philosopher—someone who studies and responds to serious problems and questions about human existence and the world

picket—to stand outside a place of work to protest a situation or try to persuade others not to enter during a strike

psychological—directed toward, influencing or acting on our minds

psychotic—exhibiting behavior that indicates a mental disorder in which thoughts and emotions are distorted

pysanky—Ukrainian Easter eggs, decorated with wax and dyes

Renaissance—a period of great change in the arts, culture, religion and philosophy between the 14th and 17th centuries

resilience—the ability to deal with and recover quickly from difficulties

sensory—of or relating to one of the senses: taste, touch, sound, sight and smell

stereotypes—ideas about people based on oversimplified opinions or prejudices

taggers—people who mark surfaces with graffiti, using their nicknames or identifying marks

transcribe—to write or type something out in a different form from the original, such as from notes or a tape recording

RESOURCES

BOOKS

Brownlee, Liz. *Shaping the World: 40 Historical Heroes in Verse.* Macmillan, 2021.

DK. *Recycle and Remake: Creative Projects for Eco Kids.* DK Children, 2020.

Hayes, Norma Jean, Ann Sayre Wiseman and John Langstaff. *Make Music! A Kid's Guide to Creating Rhythm, Playing with Sound, and Conducting and Composing Music.* Storey Publishing, 2019.

Highlights. *The Highlights Book of Things to Do: Discover, Explore, Create, and Do Great Things.* Highlights Press, 2020.

Neddo, Nick. *The Organic Artist for Kids: A DIY Guide to Making Your Own Eco-Friendly Art Supplies from Nature.* Quarry Books, 2020.

Rose, Jessica. *Let's Get Creative: Art for a Healthy Planet.* Orca Book Publishers, 2024.

Sharp, Colby. *The Creativity Project: An Awesometastic Story Collection.* Paperback edition. Little, Brown Books for Young Readers, 2019.

Stevenson, Robin. *Kid Innovators: True Tales of Childhood from Inventors and Trailblazers.* Quirk Books, 2021.

Weatherford, Carole Boston. *Dorothea Lange: The Photographer Who Found the Faces of the Depression.* Albert Whitman, 2017.

Westing, Jemma. *Out of the Box: 25 Cardboard Engineering Projects for Makers.* DK Children, 2017.

Woo! Jr. Kids Activities/Wendy Piersall. *The Drawing Book for Kids: 365 Daily Things to Draw: Step by Step.* Wendybird Press, 2017.

Youngs, Clare. *Nature Crafts for Children: 35 Step-by-Step Projects Using Found and Natural Materials.* Cico Kidz, 2023.

ONLINE

Bow Seat Ocean Awareness Programs: bowseat.org

Canadian Creativity and Innovation: canadiannetworkforimaginationandcreativity.com

The Chain Reaction Contraption Contest: chainreactioncontest.org

The Creative Museum Project: http://creative-museum.net/c/creative-museum

Directory of Online Art Galleries and Museums: refseek.com/directory/art.html

The Kindness Rocks Project: thekindnessrocksproject.com/free-downloads

Lee Edward Födi: leefodi.com

National Gallery for America's Young Inventors: nmoe.org/6/national-gallery-americas-young-inventors

Wander-Lush (a list of creative ways countries and cultures celebrate and recognize significant events in cultural and religious life): wander-lush.org/world-rituals-part-one

ACKNOWLEDGMENTS

As always, huge thanks to Douglas Brunt, my first and best reader. And to Orca editor Kirstie Hudson, who provided so much invaluable support and input on this book.

25 percent of author royalties from this book will be donated to Alexandra Neighbourhood House in Crescent Beach, British Columbia.

INDEX

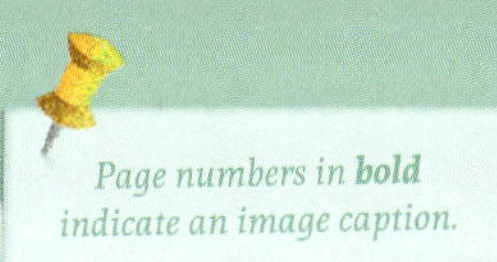

*Page numbers in **bold** indicate an image caption.*

LOUROO PHOTOGRAPHY

LOIS PETERSON

writes articles and short stories and is the author of one writing book for adults. This is her 10th children's book with Orca Book Publishers and her second nonfiction, after *Shelter: Homelessness in Our Community*. When she is not writing, teaching writing or walking on the beach, she makes art with all kinds of paper, pencils and paint. She lives on Vancouver Island.

MADELINE YEE

is a Chinese Canadian illustrator with a background in design and science, and a passion for bringing unique stories to life through visuals. She graduated from the illustration program at the Ontario College of Art and Design University in 2023. Her practice is currently based in Edmonton.

ART HAS REALLY BEEN THE WAY I HAVE BEEN ABLE TO UNDERSTAND BOTH CULTURES, AND TO UNDO THE WRONGDOING OF BOTH CULTURES.

BERNICE BING,
CHINESE AMERICAN PAINTER